"If your child has ADHD, 'normal' parenting strategies just won't work. Cindy Goldrich, with wisdom based in both experience and research, lays out the system she's created for parenting when ADHD makes it hard. She helps parents understand their ADHD children (there's more to ADHD than you think!) and how to teach them the skills they'll need to be successful in life. This book will be a revelation that you'll want to read and share again and again."

— **Sarah D. Wright**, author of
ADHD Coaching Matters: The Definitive Guide

"This book is a wise companion and personal coach for parents of children with ADHD. It's educational, confidence boosting, and filled with helpful guidance on how to give kids what they need most—acceptance, encouragement, and positive attention. Goldrich walks parents gently through the challenges and opportunities of parenting 'the child you have' and packs her book with an abundance of specialized resources. This is a must-read for parents who want the best for their child!"

— **Marilyn Price-Mitchell, PhD**, developmental psychologist

"Respected coach and educator Cindy Goldrich has written a book chock-full of excellent ideas and suggestions to help manage children with ADHD. From her rich and extensive personal and professional experience, Goldrich provides insightful concepts, strategies, and resources not readily found in other texts. This book is an outstanding resource for parents, care givers, and anyone working or living with a person with ADHD."

— **Donna Geffner, PhD, CCC-Sp/A**, Professor and Director,
St. John's University Speech and Hearing Center and
Doctoral AuD program for the Long Island Consortium

"An instruction manual for your child with ADHD! This book is a must-read for every parent who wants to help his or her child succeed, and every parent who wants peace at home. Cindy Goldrich explains the neuroscience, outlines the problems, and provides specific advice, with examples, on how to help with homework, transitions, defiance, and bedtime. She provides valuable information, whether or not your child is on ADHD medication. I will definitely recommend this book to my patients."

— **Kerry Fierstein, MD, FAAP**,
Chief Medical Officer and Pediatrician, Allied Physicians Group

8 Keys to Mental Health Series
Babette Rothschild, Series Editor

The 8 Keys series of books provides readers with brief, inexpensive, and high-quality self-help books on a variety of topics in mental health. Each volume is written by an expert in the field, someone who is capable of presenting evidence-based information in a concise and clear way. These books stand out by offering consumers cutting-edge, relevant theory in easily digestible portions, written in an accessible style. The tone is respectful of the reader and the messages are immediately applicable. Filled with exercises and practical strategies, these books empower readers to help themselves.

8 KEYS TO PARENTING CHILDREN WITH ADHD

CINDY GOLDRICH

FOREWORD BY BABETTE ROTHSCHILD

W.W. Norton & Company
New York • London

Copyright © 2015 by Cindy Goldrich

All rights reserved
Printed in the United States of America
First Edition

For information about permission to reproduce selections from this book,
write to Permissions, W. W. Norton & Company, Inc.,
500 Fifth Avenue, New York, NY 10110

For information about special discounts for bulk purchases, please contact
W. W. Norton Special Sales at specialsales@wwnorton.com or 800-233-4830

Manufacturing by R R Donnelley Harrisonburg
Production manager: Christine Critelli

Goldrich, Cindy.
8 keys to parenting children with ADHD / Cindy Goldrich ; foreword by Babette
Rothschild. — First edition.
pages cm. — (8 keys to mental health series)
Includes bibliographical references and index.
ISBN 978-0-393-71067-0 (pbk.)
1. Attention-deficit-disordered children. 2. Attention-deficit-disordered children—
Family relationships. 3. Parents of attention-deficit-disordered children. 4. Parenting.
I. Rothschild, Babette. II. Title. III. Title: Eight keys to parenting children with
ADHD.
RJ506.H9G645 2015
618.92'8589—dc23
2015017869

W. W. Norton & Company, Inc.
500 Fifth Avenue, New York, N.Y. 10110
www.wwnorton.com

W. W. Norton & Company Ltd.
Castle House, 75/76 Wells Street, London W1T 3QT

1 2 3 4 5 6 7 8 9 0

This book has been a work of love, compassion, and hope for the many people I have known who have been impacted by ADHD. I dedicate this to them: the parents, the siblings, the educators, and to those personally living with ADHD.

My love and gratitude to my husband, Steven, and my children, Carly and Ben, for their faith, support, guidance, and unconditional belief in me.

Contents

Foreword

Babette Rothschild, Series Editor

It is almost impossible to ignore the impact of attention deficit hyperactivity disorder (ADHD). Nearly daily we read about the startling number of kids who are diagnosed with it in newspapers, run across discussions online, and listen to and watch radio and television news and talk shows that expose the issue and debate treatment options. In fact, one might even suspect that the media are blowing this out of proportion. However, a close look at the facts shows that, indeed, the diagnosis of ADHD is on the rise and the overall number of children impacted is huge. According to the website of the U.S. Center for Disease Control and Prevention (CDC) on their Data and Statistics page for ADHD, the number of children diagnosed with this disorder is staggering. Currently it is estimated that more than 11% of children qualify for the diagnosis. From 1997 to 2006 rates increased an average of 3% per year; in the years 2003–2011 that grew to annual increases of 5%, affecting boys at about twice the rate of girls. Moreover, it is recognized that a significant portion of these children will carry their symptoms into adulthood. It is a major problem in schools and in homes. What are parents to do? Currently the treatment of choice is pharmaceuticals, with up to 75% of ADHD children receiving medication. And although prescription drugs have been shown to be helpful, these children also need to learn and strengthen life skills. This volume, 8 Keys to Parenting Children with ADHD, is not only timely but also a major contribution to the existing literature.

Filled with the most updated knowledge, this book offers parents a wealth of information that can help them make informed decisions about medication as well as a plethora of strategies, tools, and skills that will supplement (and in some cases possibly replace) drug treatments.

Among a wealth of wisdom herein, Goldrich's overarching mantra is "parent the child you have." It is this wisdom that sets her apart as an expert in this field. She recognizes that ADHD is not comprised of a single set of difficulties, and that every child is unique. There is no one-size-fits-all for Goldrich or in this book. She will help you to recognize the unique needs of your particular child and then support and guide you in adapting your parenting style to your child's needs. That is why Cindy Goldrich is so perfect to author this book. She has decades of experience helping parents to help their ADHD children. And she knows how to support parents through these challenges. You will feel that she, indeed, has your back.

Parents of children with ADHD face a myriad of challenges. Like all parents, they want the best for their children. But helping and guiding a child with ADHD is not an easy task. There can be times of frustration and despair, although with the proper support and guidance, there can also be enjoyment, triumph, and success—in the short term and throughout a child's life. Goldrich takes an encouraging view, identifying that ADHD primarily results from a failure of the mind's *executive function* to develop properly. Executive function describes a set of necessary cognitive skills that include our ability to make and achieve goals, exercise self-control, delay gratification, and so on. These are qualities often weak or elusive in children with ADHD. It is, therefore, that many of the strategies herein are designed to effectively strengthen the executive function. Not surprisingly, impulse control and delayed gratification (two executive function features) have been repeatedly shown to be essential skills for success in life.

Some of the earliest scientific studies of this come from Walter Mischel who, in 1970, designed an experiment to test such skills in preschoolers. Although the terminology was not in common use until decades later, these studies were really evaluating the degree of executive function in the participating children. Executive function (as will be greatly expanded on by Goldrich) is the core set of skills for any child to develop and exercise, and those with ADHD are particularly challenged in this area. What makes Mischel's research truly unique and relevant to 8 *Keys to Parenting Children with ADHD* is that he then followed his study participants for the next 40 years to see how they actually faired in their lives. The experiment, commonly known as "the marshmallow test," was very simple. A child was presented with a choice of two rewards (both favorite food items: marshmallow, pretzel, animal cookie, etc.) and asked which was preferred. The child was then told that the experimenter would be leaving the room. If the child could wait until the experimenter returned, the child would be given the preferred item. If the child rang the bell to summon the experimenter sooner, the child would be given the less preferred item. What the experimenters were intending to evaluate at the time was the kinds of mechanisms the children would use to distract their attention from the temptations so they could wait for the greater reward. Some were successful in delaying their gratification and securing their preferred item. Some were not and had to settle for the less preferred item. Because the development of executive function is central to management of ADHD and assuring a child will excel in his or her life, the marshmallow experiments are of particular interest for understanding both the skill and the deficit. And these studies further offer clues to some of the tasks that might help a child deficient in these skills to develop them as well as demonstrate the lifelong advantages of developing these early.

Mischel's research projects did not end with the initial experiments. He continued to follow the participating children for 40 years, comparing those who, as young children, were able to wait to those who were not able to wait as they moved on to adolescence and adulthood. The results of the follow-up research are tremendously relevant for all children, but especially for those with ADHD. Mischel's research further reminds us of the importance of teaching children the skills they need to delay gratification—a challenge for many children with ADHD.

Recently, media executives and child educators have realized that they can use the broad platforms of television and the Internet (particularly YouTube) to help children to better develop executive function. The following is my favorite example:

> In May 2013 *Sesame Street*, a production of the Sesame Workshop (formerly the Children's Television Workshop), released an amazingly clever, informative, and entertaining parody music video that helps kids (and adults—participants in my professional trainings *love* it!) to increase their executive function through exercising greater self-control. The video is a faithful and clever parody of Icona Pop's 2012 hit song and music video "I Love It" and features Cookie Monster struggling with a decision to postpone eating a chocolate chip cookie despite his characteristic intense craving. With song and dance, Cookie Monster and his fellow Muppet dancers and singers illustrate skills including self regulation, self-control, delayed gratification, mindfulness, and self-soothing.
> To find this video on YouTube, type "Me Want It (But Me Wait)" in the search box.

Among other features, Goldrich will help you strengthen your own executive function so that you can better manage your parenting challenges. But in addition to that, increasing the parent's executive functioning will enhance the strengthening of your child's executive functioning. It's a kind of pay-it-forward scenario. Goldrich uses her own executive function to fortify yours, and you use yours to help develop and strengthen your child's. It is with this kind of positive approach that Goldrich will help you to spin gold from what may look like straw, access silver linings, and help your children to blossom even when it appears they are stuck in mud.

Introduction

I have not failed. I've just found 10,000 ways that won't work.
— Thomas Edison

They don't mean to frustrate you. They don't want to make life so challenging and difficult, for you or for themselves.

Just as some children have trouble learning how to read, kids with ADHD often have trouble learning how to manage their attention, time, and materials. Many also have trouble tolerating frustration, being flexible, and solving their problems effectively. Just as decoding words is a learned skill, your child may need extra support learning and developing these other skills as well.

Rewards and punishments can't teach skills—but you can. It may take incredible patience, learning, understanding, investigation, and perseverance on your part, but it's worth it!

Whether we are conscious of it or not, we each have a belief about how we are supposed to parent our children—that is, of course, until our instinct or logic does not produce the results we anticipated or desired. Often, by the time parents reach out to me, they have tried many different parenting approaches and heard the advice (welcome or otherwise) of several different people. One issue we all grapple with as parents is knowing when to push our kids and when to pull back. When should we provide support, and when should we let our children manage for themselves at the risk of failing or being disappointed?

Some kids, as long as we provide a safe, nurturing environment, will generally perform as we would expect, given our guidance and a variety of appropriate opportunities along the way. However, for some kids, all the love and logic we can muster doesn't seem to be enough to help them cooperate and succeed. Why? Is it that we aren't doing it "right"? Before we begin pointing fingers and instilling guilt, I ask you to consider the nature of the child you are parenting.

Every person is born with a unique chemistry, physique, and temperament—and no operator's manual! Often, we begin to realize that we may have an especially challenging child only when we are already struggling. If you have a child who struggles because of an inability to regulate his or her attention, impulsivity, or level of activity, chances are you have become familiar with the world of ADHD.

Our journey together will begin with an overview of what ADHD is beyond the characteristics most often mentioned— impulsivity, hyperactivity, and inattentiveness. So much of what we now understand about ADHD, we have learned during the past decade or so. In fact, by the time you finish reading the first chapter, you will realize that the term *attention deficit hyperactivity disorder* really does not come close to explaining what parents and professionals truly experience with their children.

As you become more educated in and aware of how ADHD truly impacts all aspects of your child's life, you will notice a shift in the way you view and interact with your child. That will allow you to help build his or her confidence, resilence, and life skills. You will become more conscious of how you must adjust your parenting style to match the needs of your child. You may need to reframe how you think about your child and his or her actions. You may make changes in how you speak and respond to your child, and you may need to adjust how you plan and organize aspects of your home and your life.

This parenting style is what I call *"Parent the child you have,"* and it informs all the work I do as a parent coach. Family members, friends, and even well-meaning teachers and other professionals may offer advice and strategies with the intention of helping you "fix" or "teach" your child. You must learn to trust your inner voice and tailor your parenting to meet the needs of your unique child. For some, this may mean providing tighter control; for others, it may mean offering more guidance and support; and for still others, it may mean reducing certain obligations or short-term expectations. These are some of the issues I will help you explore and resolve.

For many of you, there is so much chaos, stress, arguing, and waffling that it's exhausting. Many parents wonder if their child misbehaves as a way of seeking attention. Research and experience have shown us that this is generally not the case. In fact, without effective parenting skills, many parents become trained by their children's challenging behavior—don't ask about homework, don't ask them to do chores, don't ask them to stop playing on the computer—or risk confrontation, endless frustration or constant disappointment. As we will explore more closely in the chapters ahead, children will often rely on a *behavior*, rather than a skill, in an attempt to solve a problem they perceive. For example, a child who wants candy in a store may throw a tantrum (the behavior) until his parent gives him what he wants, rather than having a rational discussion or negotiating for what he wants (using appropriate communication skills) or just dealing with not having what he wants in the moment (relying on his skill of tolerating frustration). When kids, or adults for that matter, rely on a behavior instead of skills to solve their problems, then negative, destructive patterns of behavior develop. When parents choose to ignore disruptive behavior as a way of teaching their children not to behave in this manner, generally it does little to teach kids more positive behaviors and can set them up for more severely challenging behaviors in the future.

My goal is to empower you to take charge of your parenting role in a way that protects the health and well-being of all of the members of your family. I want to help you feel confident in your decision-making regarding how you parent your challenging kid. I will help you reduce the stress and doubt you have been experiencing.

I will emphasize the ways in which you can regain order and

control as parents. "Control" is not a word many people are comfortable using in relation to parenting, as they don't want to view themselves as "overly strict." However, some parents must learn to recognize the value of being a leader and a guide to their children, as it gives their children a sense of safety, security, and confidence.

As your coach, I am going to encourage you to develop your investigative muscles. I am going to ask that you be curious, not judgmental, and try to discover the true motivation behind your child's difficult behaviors. As parents, we must understand what motivates our kids, what scares them, what their true talents are, and the different areas of their lives that need support. Only then can we develop tools and strategies that will enable us to guide them, intervene in their lives, and motivate them as they develop. We will focus on developing and strengthening effective interpersonal skills for both you and your child as a way to improve conflict resolution.

I will challenge you to take ownership for the decisions you make as a parent. You will gain confidence to act on the rules and guidelines you establish for your child on the basis of well-founded principles and consciousness. Your parenting style will be *proactive*, not *reactive* (i.e., based on your child's actions). We are going to lay a foundation for your own acceptance and trust of yourself and as well as mutual trust between you and your child. As I said in the beginning, you will learn to *"parent the child you have."*

I am going to be offering a range of parenting perspectives and techniques that I have found can dramatically improve the relationships and happiness in families. Some of the ideas will resonate more loudly and feel more comfortable for you than others, but I encourage you to give them each a try.

The statistics pointing to the hazards of undiagnosed and untreated ADHD are daunting, and they are real. The rate of divorce, incarceration, drug abuse, underemployment, and debt is much greater among individuals with ADHD than it is in the general population. However, as you will see, the potential for a uniquely magnificent life is also a real and reachable goal. As parents, your job is to look at your child's ADHD not as a curse or character flaw but as a challenge and difficulty that must be managed and an opportunity that must be explored. I believe that each child is truly *creative, resourceful,* and *whole.* His or her path may not be smooth, but the obstacles are not insurmountable. This will take time.

You will need to ignore the opinions and advice of well-meaning people who have no experience with or real knowledge of the disorder. Even today, unfortunately, not everyone is up to date on the impact of ADHD or the supports available for people with ADHD. I encourage you to refer to the resources in Appendix A for additional support and information.

All children need to know the limits of what they may and may not do, but this is all the more true for kids who have ADHD because of the additional challenges they face. Children with ADHD do not play by the same rules as other kids—for better or for worse. They will often push your buttons more than typical kids. It is not just your imagination. Their fierce independence, tenacity, and drive to question what they are expected to do will ultimately serve them well in life. As parents, you need tools to help them operate. You have been blessed with a creative, dynamic, independent thinker. This child may challenge you to question your own motives and expectations more than you may have anticipated you would be willing to. The good news—and your incentive to truly intervene—is that the brain is dynamic and continues to grow, even into adulthood. While it may take a while to see the fruits of your labor, the seeds you plant now in teaching your child tools and strategies will take root. One day when you least expect it, you will see your child doing something you taught him or her long ago that he or she had resisted doing until now.

Making lasting changes will take hard and consistent work on your part. If you are open to it, this can be a tremendous opportunity for your *own* personal growth as well. The upside will be worth it. You will have more happiness, less stress, more time, and more family warmth and connection. With *"Parent the child you have"* as your guiding principle, you will be able to help your child thrive.

The work contained in this book is based on *Calm and Connected: Parenting Children with ADHD©*. This is a seven-session workshop I developed and have facilitated with hundreds of parents through the years. The principles here are appropriate for parenting kids of all ages—until they have "launched" and are on their own. While some changes you make will be immediate, others will take time as old patterns are broken, trust is developed, and new skills are learned. I encourage you to give yourself a few days' break inbetween reading each chapter, as many of the principles and activities I will ask you to consider may take some time to think about and enact.

At the end of each chapter I will list "Guiding Thoughts." These are quotes or statements that summarize or typify the lessons within the chapter. Consider writing and posting these thoughts somewhere you can see them and set a time each day to simply reread each statement. By having just a few key thoughts to focus on, you may find it easier to remember and apply the work in this book.

I will also suggest some activities for you to do by yourself, with your parenting partner, or perhaps with your child. They will help you put into action the changes you wish to make.

Guiding Thought

Parent the child you have.

Homework

Enjoy the following poem.

THE WONDERFULNESS OF ME[1]

by Robert Tudisco

If you took all of the things that were special about me,
you could put them all together and call it AD/HD.
No better, no worse, just different that's me,
I'm really not crazy, please try and see.
Like a talented wizard in a world full of "Muggles,"
its no wonder all you see is frustration and struggles.

As I daydream and drift, you think no one's there,
but nothing could be further from the truth, believe me, I swear.
I see your impatience as my mind starts to wander
But, you don't know the depth of the thoughts that I ponder.
For creative thinkers, get lost in deep thought,
which leads to the illusion that they cannot be taught.

I know trying to reach me can give you the blues,
but I wish for just once, you could walk in my shoes.
To see things through my eyes, you would be amazed,
at the speed and sheer volume my thoughts seem to blaze.

I'm not lazy or stupid, if only you knew,
how truly difficult it is to limit myself and think like you do.
But, I can see things that you'll never see,
it's like second nature, because I am me.
With lightning fast reflexes, I can switch gears,
to be firm and inflexible is the worst of my fears.
I'm calm in a crisis and know just what to do,
For I'm in great company, Mozart, Edison and Churchill to name
just a few.

---

1. © Robert M. Tudisco, used with permission. Robert M. Tudisco is a disability attorney, author, and an adult diagnosed with ADHD.

So show me some patience, as I'm patient with you.
Just a little tolerance, it's long overdue.
Please try and understand me, along with my AD/HD,
It's a very big part of the wonderfulness of me.

8 KEYS TO PARENTING CHILDREN WITH ADHD

GET EDUCATED

How ADHD Impacts Behavior, Academics, and Social Skills

Start with wherever you are with whatever you've got.
—John Rohn

If you are seeking support for parenting your child, chances are that your journey so far has been full of challenges, worries, frustrations, and perhaps even disappointments. Now is a great time to take a moment and commit to recognizing that whatever has brought you to this place, this is just where you are now. I often hear parents express guilt, concern, and confusion regarding how they have been parenting their kids. Please know this: *Poor parenting cannot and does not cause ADHD; it is a neurodevelopmental disorder.* ADHD is real! "Although some people claim that food additives, sugar, yeast, or poor child rearing methods lead to ADHD, there is no conclusive evidence to support these beliefs" (Barkley, 1998a; Neuwirth, 1994; NIMH, 1999).[1] Harvard psychiatrist Dr. George Bush states that "ADHD is a neurobiological, neurodevelopmental disorder that is present from birth and manifests in different ways across the lifespan. While trauma or parenting can modify symptom presentation and coping, neither one plays a

---

1. Genomewide Association Studies: History, Rationale, and Prospects for Psychiatric Disorders. (2009). *American Journal of Psychiatry, 166*(5), 540–556. doi: 10.1176/appi.ajp.2008.08091354

causative role in ADHD" (personal correspondence, October 21, 2014). In fact, imaging studies show differences in the structure and activity between brains of people with and without ADHD. In people with ADHD, there is a consistent pattern of below-normal activity in the neurotransmission of the chemicals dopamine and norepinephrine in the brain's prefrontal cortex (the front part of the brain). As a result of the lower levels of dopamine, there is understimulation in the *reward* and *motivation* centers in the brain. The prefrontal cortex is thinner and matures more slowly. This does *not* imply any deficit in intelligence or ability to succeed.

So much of what we now understand about ADHD has been learned during the past decade. Few people instinctually know how to handle the atypical behavior we see in kids with ADHD. Unfortunately, most teachers and a significant number of therapists, pediatricians, and psychiatrists have not been formally educated about the academic, social, and emotional impact ADHD has on individuals throughout the life-span. Thankfully, there are many professionals who do actively seek to stay current by attending conferences and workshops and by reading scientific and research journals. It is vital that you, as your child's parent, form a team of support that includes knowledgeable experts.

When most people think about ADHD, they associate it with the main three traits of *impulsivity, hyperactivity,* and *inattentiveness.* Science and research have helped us to understand that these traits are really just the "tip of the iceberg," as author Chris Dendy says.[2] There is much more that lies beneath the surface and impacts every aspect of a person's life.

Diagnosing ADHD

While some people feel that they can easily diagnose ADHD based on simple checklists, a proper diagnosis is more complex. I recommend that you seek a professional evaluation to make sure

---

2. Ziegler Dendy, Chris & Zeigler, Alex, *A Bird's-Eye View of Life with ADD and ADHD* (Cedar Bluff, 2003), pg. 144

that you are not being swayed by incomplete or inaccurate information.

One of the questions I am often asked is, "Who can diagnose ADHD?" The answer is not as straightforward as one would hope. While any psychiatrist, pediatrician, psychologist, social worker, or nurse practitioner can technically diagnose ADHD, I strongly urge a parent to seek out someone who is specifically trained and knowledgeable about current criteria and best practices.

There is no single, objective test available to definitively diagnose ADHD. A comprehensive evaluation is necessary to make a proper diagnosis, as well as to determine if there are any coexisting conditions. An accurate diagnosis must include:

- An in-depth clinical history of both the child and the family.
- A physical exam to help rule out other possible causes of symptoms (e.g., sleep apnea, thyroid condition).
- A clinical assessment using standardized behavior rating scales or questionnaires. These forms may be completed by the child's teacher, the child's parents, or in some cases the child himself or herself. There are several respected rating scales in use today, including Conners' Rating Scale, the Vanderbilt Assessment Scales, and the Barkley Home and School Situations Questionnaires.
- An evaluation of the child's intelligence, aptitude, personality traits, or processing skills.

A complete neuropsychological or educational exam is not always necessary. If there are any concerns about learning or processing, however, I generally do recommended full testing. A neurological assessment that includes screenings of vision, hearing, verbal, and motor skills may also be recommended.

Parents are often surprised and comforted when they realize that many of the behaviors they observe in their child can be attributed to the neurobiology of ADHD. Having a complete picture of your child will help you, and your child, effectively understand and manage the challenges he or she faces as well as the strengths he or she can call upon.

What Is ADHD?

First off, some clarification: Until 1994, what we currently call ADHD was known as *attention deficit disorder* (ADD). Many still refer to it that way, especially when trying to distinguish whether a person has the "hyperactivity" component. However, as you will see, this is technically incorrect. Sadly, before 1968, this disorder was referred to as *"minimal brain dysfunction"* or *"minimal brain disorder."* Whereas previous editions of the *Diagnostic and Statistical Manual of Mental Disorders* (DSM) used by health care professionals to diagnose mental disorders included three "subtypes" of ADHD, the current DSM-5[3] now distinguishes the categories as three "presentations":

  ADHD – Hyperactive/Impulsive
  ADHD – Inattentive
  ADHD – Combined Hyperactive/Impulsive and Inattentive

A person can change "presentations" during his or her lifetime, as we often see a reduction in hyperactivity as an individual grows.

There is now a fourth category that is highly related to ADHD, although at this point researchers are still exploring whether this is a separate condition or part of ADHD itself. *"Concentration deficit disorder"* (CDD), previously referred to as *"sluggish cognitive tempo,"* describes a condition where people exhibit the functional impairments of being drowsy, lacking energy, and being readily fatigued. They may seem to daydream excessively, seem easily confused, or move very slowly. Most researchers are leaning toward categorizing CDD as a separate disorder, although there appears to be a 50% overlap between CDD and the "inattentive" type of ADHD. At this time, CDD is not yet recognized as a disorder in the DSM, and many clinicians are not yet aware of the current research.

Before I proceed to explain all the symptoms and traits of ADHD, I want to

---

3. *Diagnostic and Statistical Manual of Mental Disorders*: DSM-5, American Psychiatric Association, pgs. 59–66

caution you that there is no need to focus just on these deficits when thinking about your child. Right now you may be struggling tremendously, and these struggles are real! However, never lose sight of the fact that ADHD is just one part of who your child is. As my own daughter taught me through her work with kids with disabilities, it is important that we use *"person-first" language* to be sure we see the disability as being secondary to the person: "A person with ADHD" rather than "an ADHD person." I assure you that once we get through learning about the traits of ADHD, I will also show you the positive traits that can result as well. As you will see shortly, there are numerous successful people who are thriving in spite of, and in some senses because of, their unique brain wiring.

To be diagnosed with ADHD, at least 6 of 9 inattentive and/or hyperactive-impulsive symptoms listed in the DSM-5 must be evident in two or more settings and must be present prior to age 12. These symptoms must be present for at least 6 months. There is no requirement that the symptoms create impairment by age 12, just that they are present. For adults and adolescents age 17 or older, only 5 or more symptoms must be present for a diagnosis of ADHD. According to the Centers for Disease Control and Prevention (CDC), the rate of ADHD is 11% for kids between 4 and 17.[4] The rate of ADHD in boys is roughly double the rate in girls. The presentation in girls is often less pronounced early on, as girls tend to be more inattentive than hyperactive, which often leads to a diagnosis later in life than it is for boys. While some people outgrow or learn to manage their ADHD, 30% to 50% of adults continue to experience symptoms.[5]

ADHD has a strong genetic basis and is therefore largely hereditary (estimates are about 80%). When I begin my work with parents, it is not unusual for one parent to recognize that many of the characteristics and struggles I discuss as being related to ADHD

---

4. Centers for Disease Control and Prevention, http://www.cdc.gov/ncbddd/adhd/data.html

5. William J. Barbaresi, MDa, Robert C. Colligan, PhDb, Amy L. Weaver, MSc, Robert G. Voigt, MDd, Jill M. Killian, BSc, and Slavica K. Katusic, MDcADHD, *Mortality and Psychosocial Adversity in Adults With Childhood ADHD: A Prospective Study*, http://pediatrics.aappublications.org/content/early/2013/02/26/peds.2012-2354.abstract

remind them of their own experiences of being a kid. For some, this brings comfort and a sense of bonding. I may hear, "My daughter is a lot like I was. School was so hard and I felt so helpless. I don't want my daughter to suffer like I did." Some parents, however, have a different reaction. They feel that they "survived" and dealt with their struggles and that perhaps their child should be able to do the same. "My parents were very firm with me and I did what was expected since there was no choice. I keep telling my wife she is too soft on Jonny. It's her fault."

It is valuable to recognize that times truly are different than they were in years past. Curriculum expectations are much greater and kids are being asked to do larger quantities of difficult work at a much younger age. The requirements on their time outside school hours are much greater. There are also different social pressures, especially with the Internet and social media bringing much of what influences them outside their parents' detection and control. As you will see shortly, all of this can exacerbate the impact of ADHD and its related traits on a child, reducing his or her ability to cope and perform as he or she might have otherwise. I once had a father say to me that his own father had been very strict, and that he had spent hours and hours working but had made it through school okay. However, he felt had no relationship with his father and resented the lack of understanding and compassion he had received as a kid. Each parent needs to find their peace with how they were raised in order to face their own role and *"parent the child* they *have,"* a philosophy I presented in the Introduction.

As you will discover, the name of the condition under discussion, *attention deficit hyperactivity disorder,* is rather misleading. In fact, there are many in the field who would like to rename ADHD so it more accurately reflects the true nature of this disorder. I will mention some of these names as I explain the different components of ADHD.

Is It an Attention Deficit?

One of the greatest misconceptions about ADHD is that it renders a person unable to pay attention. In fact, many parents contact me and say, "He can't have ADHD! He can spend hours at the video games when he wants to!" What science has taught us is that because of the below-normal activity in the neurotransmission of dopamine and norepinephrine, some people struggle *regulating* their attention, leading some professionals to suggest that we rename ADHD "deficits in attention regulation disorder." People with ADHD can pay attention, but not always *when* they need to, for *as long* as they need to, or on *what* they need to—especially when they are not interested or internally motivated. Sometimes, when a person is very interested in what he or she is focused on (such as playing a video game or building with blocks), the individual is actually "*hyperfocused.*" This means that the person is deeply and intensely focused to the point that he or she has shut out other thoughts or stimuli. This is why very often people with ADHD have a hard time *transitioning* from one task to another. I will talk about strategies to help kids with transitioning from one task or activity to another in Key 6.

At other times, when people with ADHD are bored or uninterested, they struggle to stay tuned in to the current topic and resist more stimulating thoughts. Many people with ADHD are actually often *multi-focused*, paying attention to many things at the same time at the expense of directed attention to one thought. They may even feel that they have a "bombardment" of thoughts, making it difficult to focus on any one task. This raises the importance of understanding the science of ADHD. When the brain does not produce enough dopamine, the brain actually struggles to make the connections and stay alert. If a child is having trouble paying attention to the task at hand, sitting still may actually increase the difficulty he or she is experiencing. Movement can help stimulate the networks of the brain that control attention.

I once observed a child who was continuously roaming the

classroom (with the permission of the well-informed teacher) while his teacher lectured. When the teacher asked this child a question directly related to her presentation, the child was spot on with the answer.

Strategies for Improving Focus at Home and at School

Since movement is not always practical or desirable, many people succeed in focusing by holding and manipulating an object. This is commonly referred to as "fidgeting." Allow your child to hold an item (a "fidget") that he or she can quietly, discretely manipulate. This item can be anything from a piece of felt to a rubber toy or a ring. Have a variety of objects available at home and at school. It is important to help your child to distinguish between "fidgeting" and "playing." To "fidget" means to passively manipulate the object in the background, secondary to the task at hand. To "play" means to focus primarily on the object and interact with it. Also, teach your child that he or she must not distract others with his or her fidgeting. Sometimes a little investigating, open-mindedness, creativity, and patience can go a long way in helping kids learn how they function best.

OTHER TIPS:
- Allow your child to move around within reason. Sitting on an exercise ball chair or even a rolled-up sweatshirt can provide the right stimulation to help your kid stay engaged in his or her work.
- Allow your child the freedom to stand up while working, just as an adult often does. This can be done in the classroom as well with the teacher's prior approval.
- Music is another great form of stimulation. Let your child experiment with different genres — it need not be classical to effective. It may be helpful to prepare (in advance) a playlist of songs your child finds are effective without creating too much distraction.
- Interactive games for learning facts can be stimulating and fun at the same time. Next time your child needs to memorize vocabulary words, for example, play a game of catch; toss the ball as you

say each word and have your child toss it back as he or she responds. Or play a game of concentration: Make two sets of flash cards—one with the word, a second with the definition. Lay them all out facedown and find the matching pair.

Impulsivity

By the time I think about what I'm gonna do . . . I already did it!

—Dennis the Menace

Interrupting, blurting out, grabbling things, throwing things . . . These poor kids—they don't always mean to be bad—it's part of their neurobiology. Their brain often operates by the motto "Ready, fire . . . aim." Also, due to lower levels of the dopamine that provides natural reinforcement for the brain, many people with ADHD engage in more risky behaviors to seek high stimulation. Helping kids manage their impulsivity is one of the greatest challenges parents and professionals face. While they may not always be in control of their impulses, kids with ADHD do need to learn to manage as best they can and to be responsible for their actions. As I will discuss shortly, one of the possible supports can be appropriate medication. However, regardless of that choice, there are other steps you can take to help your child become more aware and curb some of his or her natural impulsivity.

Strategies for Managing Impulsivity

The greatest challenge comes in helping kids catch themselves in the moment just *before* they take action. Here are some ways to help them develop both awareness and skills for stopping behavior before it is too late.

- Teach your child phrases (such as "May I add . . .") that will help them know how and when they can interrupt to join a conversa-

tion or share a comment. Give them a chance to practice this
during family conversations, such as during mealtime or driving
time, to give them the experience of interrupting with and without visual cues.

- Have a private signal that lets them know to "Wait, Think, and
then Go." The signal should be discreet but distinctive so that
you can use it with play dates or in public.
- Especially if your child is younger, make sure he or she knows
the rules and expectations for games and gatherings. Discussing
strategies beforehand can help children plan what to do in challenging situations.
- Collaborate with your child's teacher so that you are each using
the same strategies and language to prevent and correct actions.
- Help your child learn to recognize his or her thoughts and
choose not to act on them. For instance, your child might realize, "I'm really bored waiting, but I can do it longer without getting in trouble." Or, "I'm angry that he has the ball, but I can ask
for it or wait my turn."

Hyperactivity

When I think of children with ADHD, I like to think of Tigger
from Winnie the Pooh. Sometimes kids with ADHD have boundless energy that can overwhelm or create havoc for everyone
around. It's as if there's an internal motor that won't stop. And it
seems to be at its peak when boredom or stress are involved. Kids
who are hyperactive tend to be identified earlier on by teachers and
parents. A good clinical assessment can help distinguish between
a very active child and a "hyperactive" child.

A Poor Sense of Time

Do you ever notice that your child gets ready to go way too early or
way too late? One thing that constantly frustrates most parents of

kids with ADHD is that it seems their kids have *no sense of time.* They are constantly trying to move their kids along, hurry them up, or get them to focus on the task at hand. Well, the reality is, they *don't* in fact have an accurate sense of time. Research shows that the performance of kids with ADHD in accurately estimating different time intervals is weaker than in kids without ADHD and does not improve when they are tested on medication.[6] They have difficulty judging the passage of time or how long something might take to accomplish.

Time is NOW . . . and NOT NOW.

That paper that's due on Friday . . . that's not now, so why are you talking about it? Aunt Susan is coming over tonight and you want me to clean up . . . that's not now, so what's the rush? People with ADHD live so much in the moment that they often act without calling upon past experiences and lessons or without regard to potential consequences for the future. All that exists for them is the present. Soon and later are not now, so they are not considered. People with ADHD have a difficult time keeping future goals and consequences in mind. They do not seem to benefit from warnings about what is going to happen later.

Strategies to Make Time Real

Have clocks and timers in several locations in your home, especially the bathroom, the bedroom, the kitchen, and wherever there is a television or play area. Many kids, while they are adept at reading an analog clock, relate more successfully to a digital clock that has a specific number.

Whenever you ask your child to do something during a specific time period—for example, to come down for dinner in 5 minutes—you must give him or her some tool or strategy to help. An excellent resource is a "Time Timer," which can be purchased

---

6. Dr. Russell Barkley, *Journal of the International Neuropsychological Society* (July 1997), pgs. 359–369

in a variety of sizes from several online outlets. This is a simple one-hour clock that provides a visual representation of time passing. You or your child moves a dial to set it a certain number of minutes, and that amount of time will appear in red. As time passes, only the red portion is visible, showing how much time remains.

Another strategy is to ask your child the current time and then tell him the time you expect him to be somewhere. This will help him notice the current time and help him be accountable for the time he is expected to transition to another activity.

Executive Function Deficits

During the past few years, there has been increased attention paid to *executive function*, the set of mental skills or processes that have to do with managing oneself and one's resources in order to achieve a goal. They are the self-regulating skills that we all use every day to accomplish just about everything. You can think of *executive function skills* as different managers in your brain, and you are the chief executive officer (CEO) who is in charge of making sure each manager is well trained and has the support and supplies they need at all times.

Executive functions are the located in the prefrontal cortex of the brain (the front part of the brain), and they start developing during infancy. Figure 1.1 is a chart showing each of the *executive function skills* areas.

As you learn about the different *executive function* areas, you may notice that your child is behind in several or even most of these skills relative to his or her peers. In fact, several experts now refer to ADHD as an *executive function disorder*. It seems you cannot have ADHD without having *executive function* deficits. This is another reason that the name *ADHD* is not sufficiently descriptive, so perhaps naming the disorder "*deficits in executive function skills*" would be more accurate (although you *can* have *executive function* disorder without having ADHD).

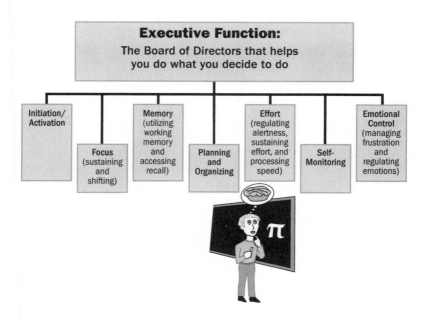

Fig. 1.1 Executive Function Skills

Typically, *executive function skills* are fully developed by about 25 to 30 years of age. While kids with ADHD may be intellectually typical, research has shown that for people with ADHD, these skills may develop up to 30% more slowly. There are many things you will learn to do as you read this book to actively support your child's *executive function skills*. I have included some basic tips here to help illustrate each of the skills.

Initiation/Activation

Did you ever notice that your child might have a hard time just getting started? She may be aware of what she needs to do, but she may have a hard time taking the first step—she just can't seem to start her engine. Keep in mind that most people with ADHD truly do have a sort of "time blindness" where they often don't feel urgency until the "fire is at the door," so to speak.

Tip: Help your child notice the struggle she is having getting started on routine activities by gently commenting, without criticizing. You might begin by engaging her with a neutral, nonjudgmental statement of observation: "I notice you are (…working on your math, playing with your blocks, just hanging out)". This personal connection can help you more easily signal that it's time to transition. They you can try some of these strategies:

Help her do the first step—sometimes kids just need to gather momentum and your presence at the beginning can help.

Help her develop a short routine that signals to her—"It's start time." This can be setting up the desk, setting a timer, doing 5 jumping jacks, etc.

Have her set a timer at an agreed upon time to signal, "It's start time."

If possible, help her anticipate how long the activity will last so that she gets a sense that it *will end*. Sometimes knowing an activity is finite makes it easier to get started.

Focus: Sustaining and Shifting

People with *executive function* deficits truly have a hard time screening out other stimuli. Background noises, thoughts, and visual stimuli can each pull them away from the task at hand. They can get drawn away so easily, and then they have a hard time pulling themselves back to where they were. This is why they seem to misplace or forget things so often.

As I mentioned earlier, the opposite, "hyperfocus," can also occur, as when a person becomes locked into one thought or activity and totally loses track of other stimuli. Both of these challenges contribute to making shifting or transitioning smoothly from one activity to another difficult.

Tip: Be willing to sit with your child as he works on a specific task or activity. Yes, even your teen may need you nearby while he does his homework. This is called being a "body double." Your presence acts as a "grounding rod" to keep him on task and focused. This is not meant to be punitive but rather supportive. Remember, it's not always within their conscious control to focus.

Utilizing Working Memory

Working memory is the "mental workspace" where we store, recall, and manipulate information, facts, and ideas. Deficits in working memory can impact many aspects of learning, including comprehension, computation, memorizing, and multiple-step procedures. This is also part of the reason why your child may seem lost when you say, "Could you please go to your room and get your shoes and your backpack and get my book from my room?" She just can't hold on to all that information and act on it as well. She may also struggle to summarize information or recall details without support.

Tip: When remembering is required (for multiple-step activities or keeping track of characters or concepts in a book, for instance), encourage your child to keep scratch paper to jot down basic notes. Also, when possible, posts schedules and to-do lists where they are most useful.

Planning and Organizing

Effective planning requires being able to appropriately anticipate future events. This requires an accurate understanding of time. Effective organization of materials requires a person to apply structure or a system in a methodical and systematic manner, requiring sustained focus and attention.

Tip: Provide a variety of organizational options and encourage your child to learn what works best for his particular style. Also, help your child work backwards from a future goal to create smaller tasks that can be planned in the present.

Regulating Alertness, Sustaining Effort, and Adjusting Processing Speed

Staying tuned in can be a real challenge when extended attention is needed, especially without a change in the presentation of material or stimuli. People with *executive function* deficits may find themselves actually drowsy when not sufficiently stimulated.

I liken it to a windup doll that needs constant rewinding. Additionally, they may suffer from a slower than typical *processing speed*. This is the pace of completing a task (responding, reflecting, reacting) reasonably accurately. Some of this challenge may be due to the struggles people with ADHD have in utilizing their weaker working memory as well, making it difficult to respond with ease.

A slower-than-average processing speed can create one of the greatest hurdles for your child. Realizing that some kids have a slower processing speed helps explain why it seems to take longer for them to respond or react to questions or requests. It's not necessarily that they are defying you—they may just need longer to process what is happening. The hard part for you as the parent is that it means you may need to adjust *your* pace and expectation to allow your child ample time to process and perform. Rushing your child will often exacerbate the problem, creating stress and overwhelm. This is also the reason that some students receive accommodations in school, allowing for extended time for tests. (See Appendix B for explanations of an IEP and a 504 plan.)

Tip: Provide breaks during longer activities whenever possible. Also, allow movement, snacks, and music to keep the brain stimulated and alert. And be patient! Allow extra time for responding.

Self-Monitoring

Often parents express concern that their child does not seem to notice when she is off task, or that she is perhaps not "in tune" with what is happening socially. Your child may not notice how she is impacting another child or how that other child perceives her and therefore may not adjust her behavior appropriately. Your child may also have trouble pacing herself during an activity and may move too quickly or too slowly. Some of these challenges are related to impulsivity and distractibility. Additionally, your child may not be engaged in helpful "self-talk." This is sometimes referred to as *metacognition*, or, simply, thinking about what you are thinking about. Noticing yourself in action and talking to yourself are required for making necessary corrections of your own behavior and completing goals.

Tip: Use imaginary play or watching television shows to discuss how people are being perceived and how they are imagining how others are feeling and thinking. Also, be willing to volunteer your own thought process as you go about your day planning, organizing, and reacting to situations.

Emotional Control

When reviewing the diagnostic criteria for ADHD, there is not much mention of managing emotions. Medical papers dating back to 1798 had always included emotion in the conceptualization of ADHD. This continued up to the 1968 edition of the DSM-II. Since then, emotional dysregulation has been excluded from the clinical conceptualization of the condition. Yet, more than the impulsivity, distractibility, and hyperactivity, this *executive function* area creates more stress and challenge for both the child and those with whom he or she interacts. In fact, Dr. Russell Barkley, preeminent researcher in the field of ADHD, has suggested that "*deficits in emotional self-regulation*" is another more appropriate name for ADHD.[7] People with *executive function* deficits can be emotionally impulsive and may have a hard time:

- Inhibiting their initial reaction or response
- Regulating, modulating, and monitoring their level of anger and expression of raw emotion
- Being patient
- Tolerating frustration
- Refocusing their attention away from an event or toward an event that might encourage a more positive, acceptable mood
- Self-soothing, regaining composure, or calming down

You may find that your child gives up very easily without persisting past a challenge or struggle. This can make all aspects

---

7. Dr. Russell Barkley, Keynote Address, National CHADD Conference, 2012

of life more challenging, especially learning and long, complex activities.

Addressing the Potential for Social Rejection

Some children who have ADHD struggle when it comes to social interactions. They may have a difficult time taking turns, respecting personal boundaries, and controlling their emotional reactions. Dr. Barkley states, "The single biggest predictor of social rejection among kids and adults with ADHD is not distractibility, inattentiveness . . . [or] their hyperactivity—it is their inability to regulate their frustration, impatience, hostility and anger."[8] Remember, ADHD is a neurologically based problem of *emotional regulation*.

Tip: Learning to pause, reflect, and react appropriately is not an easy lesson to learn. I will be discussing strategies for self-regulation skills, starting with the next chapter and building with each chapter. For now, just build up your reservoir of empathy and patience. Help is on the way.

Strategies for Building Executive Function Skills at Home

It is very valuable to teach your child about *executive function* skills. Let him know that he is capable of developing expert "managers" for each of the skill areas. Help him discover the tools and strategies he needs to be the best CEO of his brain. When you do activities with him, try to ask questions and let him do the muscle work, rather than telling him the steps yourself. For example, packing for a trip can be an entire learning experience. Even a toddler can be actively involved in the process:

- "How will you know what to wear? Think about the weather, the activities, the space for packing . . . "

---

8. Dr. Russell Barkley, Keynote Address, National CHADD Conference, 2012

- "What is the best way to pack? What size suitcase will you need? Who will be carrying it? How are you traveling?"
- Have your child lay out all the items he wants, and then pack the suitcase together as you help him discover how to organize the items best.

Other great activities for developing executive function skills include planning a meal, building with blocks, imaginary play, gardening, and organizing a playroom, to name a few.

Coexisting Conditions

One half to two thirds of all children with ADHD have at least one coexisting condition.[9] A few of the most common are described below.

Learning Disabilities

Twenty-five to fifty percent of children with ADHD have some form of learning disability, primarily in the areas of reading, written expression, or math. This is why it is often advised that an educational evaluation accompany any assessment for ADHD.

When you consider the steps involved in writing, you will realize that it is a very complex venture. Think of each *executive function* involved as well as the other challenges we have mentioned. Holding a thought, organizing thoughts, recalling spelling and grammar rules, focusing on the paper, and other concerns are involved in the process.

Many children with ADHD also have poor handwriting. Sloppy handwriting is not necessarily just a physical challenge requiring occupational therapy; however, if it is a particular problem, a trained occupational therapist may be able to offer

---

9. ADHD and Co-Existing Disorders, http://help4adhd.org/en/treatment/coexisting/WWK5

some support. Learning how to type using proper keyboarding techniques (as opposed to being efficient on a smartphone or tablet) is now more crucial than ever. This skill will be especially important if your child receives the accommodation allowing him or her to use word processing during homework and tests. I recommend teaching proper keyboarding by second or third grade.

Some children can qualify for formalized accommodations, modifications, and/or support services through their school by having an individualized education plan (IEP) or a 504 plan. (For information regarding these plans, see Appendixes B and D.)

Difficulty Falling Asleep and/or Waking Up

Twenty-five to fifty percent of children with ADHD struggle with sleep habits.[10] There are many reasons this occurs outside of the potential side effects of stimulant medications. Some children experience a bombardment of thoughts as they lie in bed, making drifting off to sleep seem impossible. Also, their circadian rhythm (the roughly 24-hour cycle that regulates sleep) may be atypical. You may find that your child is like a bear in winter when you try to wake him or her. There are actually alarm clocks that are especially made for extremely deep sleepers (e.g., Clocky, Sonic Bomb, Ramos); however, I caution you that on some level your child must be motivated if he or she is to respond to *any* alarm.

Tip: Melatonin, a hormone naturally produced by the body, helps control your sleep and wake cycles. Artificial light from computer, tablet, and phone screens at night may reduce melatonin levels. In a study published in the journal *Applied Ergonomics*, researchers found that two hours of exposure to a bright tablet

---

10. Sleep Problems Common in Children with ADHD, http://www.reuters.com/article/2009/03/26/us-sleep-adhd-idUSTRE52P7ED20090326

screen at night reduced melatonin levels by about 22 percent.[11] Be sure to limit screen time before bed. Apparently, even wearing sunglasses while looking at the screens may help reduce the impact of the blue light. Also, check with your child's doctor to see if perhaps melatonin supplements might be recommended to help him or her fall asleep.

Depression

Thirty percent of children with ADHD have coexisting depression.[12] It is important to recognize that depression can sometimes look like anger or aggression. The challenges one faces by having ADHD, especially when it has gone undiagnosed or untreated, can create depression. However, there seems to be a clinical basis for the depression as well. It is very important while seeking treatment that the impact of one condition be considered while treating the other condition. Generally, psychiatrists recommend treating the depression first so as to make it easier to manage the ADHD symptoms.

Substance Abuse

Between 5 and 40 percent of people with ADHD abuse some form of drugs. This wide range reflects the difference between those who have been effectively treated and learned how to manage their ADHD and those who have not. Untreated ADHD is also associated with higher rates of alcohol use. Research suggests that successful treatment of ADHD in childhood appears to prevent substance abuse later in life. It is hypothesized that those who were not properly treated for their ADHD during childhood may, in fact, self-medicate with drugs and/or alcohol.

---

11. Anahad O-Connor, Really? Using a Computer Before Bed Can Disrupt Sleep, http://well.blogs.nytimes.com/2012/09/10/really-using-a-computer-before-bed-can-disrupt-sleep/?_php=true&_type=blogs&_php=true&_type=blogs&_r=1, Sept. 10, 2012

12. ADHD and Comorbidity, http://www.medscape.org/viewarticle/418740

Oppositional Defiant Disorder (ODD)

Here the statistic is quite large: About 40 percent of kids with ADHD also have ODD. Children with ODD exhibit angry, violent, and disruptive behaviors toward their parents, caretakers, and other authority figures; chronic aggression; frequent outbursts; and a tendency to argue, ignore requests, and engage in intentionally annoying behavior. For many parents, these behaviors, more than the academic struggles and challenges with time management, organization, and inattentiveness, create the greatest stress and discord in family dynamics and relationships.

Many people, including Dr. Russell Barkley, believe that ODD is actually a *potential* (rather than a coexisting condition) as a result of the condition of ADHD, especially for those with either hyperactivity/impulsivity or combined presentations. People with ADHD, especially those with impulsivity, are often very quick to express their emotions. When you look closely at the diagnostic criteria of the DSM-5 for ODD, you will see that the need for *emotional self-regulation* is mentioned in seven of the eight symptoms. It is believed that this contributes to ODD behaviors.

A special note to moms: It is very important that your sons view you as capable and assertive. They will need to know that you can handle their reactions and that you will set boundaries and not just wait for Dad to enforce the rules. One day they may be bigger and stronger than you, and you must be able to control them with your words.

Anxiety

Forty to fifty percent of kids with ADHD suffer from anxiety, including obsessive-compulsive disorder (OCD).[13] It is important to understand the role and presence of anxiety in youth. The amygdala is a region in the brain that is critical in evaluating and

---

13. Roberto Olivardia, *ADHD and Anxiety*, http://www.add.org/BlankCustom.asp?page=ADHDandAnxiety

responding to fear. It sends and receives information to our prefrontal cortex, alerting us to danger even before we have time to think about it—for example, when we hear a sudden noise or see a large bug. The prefrontal cortex, where the *executive function* resides, can help us reason and evaluate to assess the actual risk and respond appropriately. Since the prefrontal cortex is one of the last brain regions to mature, adolescents have far less ability to modulate emotions. However, as kids mature, the anxiety often dissipates.

I do find that the impact of anxiety is often very significant in creating challenges for a child with ADHD. Anxiety can prevent a child from participating, initiating work, trying new strategies, and thinking clearly. Also, without proper coping techniques to manage their anxiety, children who are experiencing anxiety will do what they can to reduce that feeling—which often is to push off or away the object, or person, associated in their mind with creating that stress. This, I believe, is a major contributing factor to the development of *oppositional defiant disorder*. In the chapters that follow, I will be focusing on how to help reduce the impact that anxiety has on your child's behavior and performance.

What Else Is Part of ADHD?

Performance Inconsistency

"If he did it once, why can't he always do it?" Often I hear parents and teachers express frustration at the inconsistent performance of a child with ADHD. You may become exasperated when your child repeatedly makes the same errors in judgment or action or fails to do what you know he or she is more than capable of doing. A helpful expression I use often in dealing with this quandary is, "ADHD is not a problem of knowing what to do, but rather a problem of doing what you know." It is the "when," "where," and "how," not just the "what," that needs to be tended to. ADHD is *not* a challenge of intelligence. In fact, an extremely high number of people with ADHD have higher-than-average intelligence, with many being considered "twice exceptional" (intellectually gifted kids who have some form of disability). While your child may at times appear lazy or unmotivated, often, as we will explore later on, there is much more going on. Neuropsychologist Samuel Goldstein found that "twenty-five percent of the explanation for performance on all kinds of measures, including IQ tests, is predicted not by how much you know but by how you demonstrate what you know."[14] So much has to do with the strategies used. Think of the *executive function* skills and other challenges children face as being stars in their brain. When kids are struggling to perform, as it seems they can or should, I like to say that it's as if all the stars in the universe are not lined up properly.

Sensitivity to the Physical Environment

Very often I find that children with ADHD are especially bothered by the tag on their shirt, the line of their sock, and so forth. They also may be especially tactile and enjoy wearing their hoody sweatshirt even when the weather does not call for it. My suggestion is to believe that their concern is real for *them*, just as we each experience temperature differently. Trying to convince a child that the line on the sock is "not a big deal" and that she should get used to it gives her the message that she is not understood or believed.

What Does It Feel Like to Have ADHD?

Think of your child's brain as a city with streets and avenues that carry traffic. The streets are neuron pathways and the traffic is all the information, sensory inputs, impulses, feelings, and instructions that the brain has to process. For some kids, the traffic lights are not in sync. There are chemicals in the brain called neurotransmitters that help brain cells communicate with each other. In

---

14. Samuel Goldstein, *Learning and the Brain Conference*, 2013

some people, these neurotransmitters do not communicate well with one another. It's as if the traffic signals that regulate traffic in the brain are not working. Let's say it's Friday afternoon at rush hour in your city, and the traffic lights go out. What is the result? Gridlock, traffic jams, frustration, chaos. This is what is going on in your child's head. You can also think about your child's brain as being just like his bedroom. All the clothes and stuff he owns is in that bedroom, but it's anyone's guess where things are. Clothes may be under the bed, buried under large piles, hanging out the dresser drawers, stuffed in the closet. When your child needs to access information in his brain, it's up there. It just may take a while to find it.

This is also why some kids may appear to be so controlling—they don't feel in control of their internal thoughts and actions, so they try to control what they can around them. This internal chaos also contributes to their difficulty with transitions, new situations, and sudden changes.

Kids, and some adults, seek stimulation to keep the traffic cop awake in their brains, even if it is negative behavior creating the stimulation. Did you ever notice that out of the blue, your child might start bugging his or her siblings or just creating havoc? Imagine now how hard it must be for some kids to sit still in class when they are bored with the material and their brain is in chaos. This is why so many of our kids come home from school mentally taxed and just plain tired. They have to work so hard to stay alert when things are not innately stimulating. This is also why projects don't get finished once the interesting parts are completed.

What Messages Does the World Give Kids Who Have ADHD?

Very often it is the unspoken messages that kids receive that can be the most damaging to their confidence and self-esteem. I have often heard school personnel say that "all children are treated equally" and that "no child is made to feel uncomfortable because of any learning differences or ADHD." Unfortunately, while that may be their intention, my practice is filled with parents and kids who have had quite a different experience.

For example, when David's new friend found out he was in Resource Room, his friend said, "But I thought you were smart"— mistakenly assuming that anyone needing support could not be intelligent. After staying up all night to study for a math test only to fail it, Sam was told by his teacher that he just needed to "try harder." When Sarah worked hard to organize the game in a way that helped her manage her anxiety, her friend told her that she was being "too controlling and bossy." After asking the basketball coach to explain, yet again, the play the team was being asked to practice, Michael was told he was "too much trouble" and needed to "pay better attention."

Without self-awareness, coping strategies, and often, sheer gumption, facing the world each day can be a daunting task for a child with ADHD.

Sibling Relationships

Having a child with ADHD can greatly impact the dynamics between and among siblings. You may find that you spend considerable time supporting or monitoring your child who has ADHD. Helping with homework, doctor's appointments, redirecting, and sometimes, disciplining can take time away from the other children in the family. Further complicating the situation for the other children is that some kids with ADHD may be sources of overwhelm, annoyance, or embarrassment—either within the family or during outside events or gatherings.

Tip: When possible, help the other children understand some of the challenges your child with ADHD faces. Be sure to balance your discussion by showing how *all* people have different traits that may be challenging, and be sure to highlight your child's strengths as well as challenges. Teach all your children that "fair" does not mean "equal." "Fair" means giving each person what he or she needs; just because one person gets glasses doesn't mean that each person needs glasses to see properly. Try your best to find time to balance the time you spend with each of your kids. Also, be aware of the potential burden your child with ADHD may place on your other children and discuss coping strategies and boundaries with each of them.

Medication: Know the Facts

Whether or not you decide to give your child medication to help him or her manage the symptoms of ADHD, it is important to understand the potential impact of your decision. I recommend speaking with a professional who is current and expert in the field of ADHD medication. While this is never a decision to be rushed, having the correct information and resources is very valuable. You will want to work with someone who recognizes that medication is only a part of the overall treatment plan and helps you collaborate to create the proper team.

As I mentioned initially, research shows that there is a lower level of activity in the neurotransmission of the chemicals dopamine and norepinephrine in the brain's prefrontal cortex. This is the region of the brain that is associated with emotional regulation, working memory, attention, decision making, organization, and impulsivity. ADHD medications are stimulants that incite the underactive part of the brain, increasing the levels of dopamine and norepinephrine. This is why when children with ADHD (who already seem overstimulated) take stimulant medications, they are more able to function on par with kids who don't have ADHD and whose chemistry is already in balance.

Many parents are understandably reluctant to begin giving their children medication, especially at a young age. In fact, most parents who contact me are looking for ways to avoid using medication. My experience and belief is this: Parent education, support, and involvement, along with creating a comfortable, compassionate, and supportive school environment, are the most crucial ingredients for helping a child learn to master his or her ADHD traits and be successful in life. Having said that, due to the brain chemistry of children with ADHD and the challenges most kids face in paying attention when necessary and in moderating and managing their emotional responsiveness, proper ADHD medication can be not only helpful, but necessary and life enhancing. This is a very personal and difficult decision; however, there is support to suggest that perhaps medication should be considered, at least on a trial basis.

Stimulant medications such as amphetamines and methylphenidate have been used to treat ADHD since 1937. Ritalin and the other stimulants used for ADHD have been found to be effective for approximately 80 percent of children. And research has found that children are "neither more likely nor less likely to develop alcohol and substance-use disorders as a result of being treated with stimulant medication."[15]

Because the effectiveness of ADHD medications is not dependent on a person's age or weight, the proper formula and dose may take some trial and error. There are several new formulas and methods of dispensing the medication, so it is vital to see a professional who keeps up with the current research and literature. It may take up to six months to find and reach the proper regimen, so if you are exploring using medication, be patient and persistent. Be sure to keep a log of what medication your child is taking, the dose, and his or her reaction (impact on appetite, sleep, mood, attentiveness, and other areas you are concerned about).

Proper ADHD medication can help do the following:

- Improve focus and attention regulation
- Improve working memory and processing speed
- Reduce hyperactivity and impulsivity
- Reduce irritability and obsessiveness

---

15. Stuart Wolpert, *Are children who take Ritalin for ADHD at greater risk of future drug abuse?*, http://newsroom.ucla.edu/releases/are-children-who-take-ritalin-246186, May 19, 2013

- Reduce disruptive, aggressive, and noncompliant behavior
- Lead to greater acceptance by peers

Remember, ADHD is a condition caused by a chemical imbalance in the brain; it is not a voluntary choice. It is very important to recognize that *pills don't teach skills!* They just make it easier for people to learn and regulate their emotions and actions. If you as a parent are not committed to setting boundaries, enforcing rules, maintaining high expectations, and recognizing your child's efforts, ADHD medications will accomplish little.

When to Start Medication

While most parents want to avoid giving their kids medication at a very young age, there are times when it may be warranted. For some children, being able to pay appropriate attention in school is so painfully challenging that they miss out on developing the building blocks that are the foundation of a good education. Researchers found that children with attention problems showed slower growth in learning new material in reading and math than others, even those with aggressive behavior. Addressing attention problems in early childhood will help many kids make academic gains throughout their school careers, so using ADHD stimulant medication early on may be justified.

For some children, the impulsivity and hyperactivity are so intense that they may cause accidental harm to themselves or others. Very young kids may have no sense of fear or danger when it comes to running, jumping, throwing, and so forth. Proper medication may help them pause enough to act more safely. Some kids also suffer socially as they struggle to take turns in games and conversations, notice other's needs and interests, and balance their own impulses in order to fit in with others. Medication can help children be more available to learn and adjust to social situations and feel more successful gaining and maintaining friendships.

Some parents feel that they need to have their kids take the medication only during school days. Keep in mind that ADHD affects all aspects of life: school, home, social life, extracurricular activities, and so forth. Just as you need to be able to focus and regulate your emotions in school, you need to be able to concentrate and regulate yourself in other areas of life to be successful. Some kids find that they are more successful in their sports or in pursuing their other extracurricular interests when they take their medication. You, and your child, may find that a consistent daily medication regimen is best, regardless of the school calendar.

When to Tell Your Child About ADHD

Parents often wonder if, when, and how to tell their kids that they have ADHD. I always tell parents that this is a very individual decision. However, there are a few things to consider:

- If your child is being tested for ADHD and is aware that not all kids go through such testing, she may be concerned or upset. You may want to explain that it seems she is struggling (with learning, staying still when she needs to, paying attention, etc.) and that you want to help her see why this is the case and what might help. Try to give specific examples to support your concern and be as nonjudgmental and noncritical as possible.
- If you are going to be giving your child medication, you want to help her understand as much as possible why she is taking the medication. Not only will this help her accept the medication, but it can also allow her to provide valuable feedback to you and the doctor prescribing the medication.
- Most kids, by the time they reach about 10 or 11 years old, have heard someone in school, on TV, or in a movie mention ADHD— and, unfortunately, often not in the most positive way. Additionally, for those children who have access to a computer and have learned how to search the Internet, there is tons of information— some factual and supportive, some misleading and potential detrimental—out there to explore. Just as with other touchy and

important issues we must discuss with our kids, educating them about ADHD is usually best coming from loving parents who can more appropriately "control the narrative" and be there to answer questions and concerns. You might start by just asking what they already know and then being prepared to present them with a balanced, encouraging picture that empowers them to find their own best way of facing their personal challenges. The next section as well as the chapters ahead will give you plenty of support in helping your child achieve that goal.

When the Parent Has ADHD, Too

Parenting a child when you have ADHD yourself often creates additional challenges. It can be challenging to organize and manage others when you are struggling to keep organized in your own life. Getting proper treatment for your own ADHD (which might include medication, cognitive behavioral therapy, or ADHD coaching) can greatly impact the success and satisfaction you will have in raising your kids.

Your Perspective—and Why Does It Matter?

By now you may be feeling a bit overwhelmed or saddened by some of the challenges your child has been facing. In my workshops, many parents express regret or even guilt at some of the ways they have spoken or interacted with their kids. I've heard comments such as:

- "I just assumed he was lazy. I see now he has really tried hard and just wasn't able to keep all the thoughts in his head at one time."
- "I made such a big deal over his messy room that I didn't realize the stress it was causing all of us."
- "My dad pushed me so hard I figured that's what I had to do, but it's not working and we fight all the time. I don't think my way makes sense now that I understand more about ADHD."

- "I was putting all the pressure on my son to change, not realizing how much of the struggle was because of *how*, *what*, and *when* we were expecting him to accomplish things. I see we need to make some changes on our end as well."

How you see your child is going to be the most important factor in the success of your efforts on his behalf. These school years may be very difficult for your child. His teachers and his peers may tell him in a variety of ways that somehow he is not good enough. Other people often determine how many successful experiences kids have each day. It is important to realize, and make sure those who work with your child understand, that even when he appears to be just sitting around and ignoring his responsibilities, he is not lazy. Often he is operating out of fear, avoidance, or skills deficits. Sometimes he just can't get his brain to focus, no matter what the incentive and how badly he wants it. As frustrating as this may be to watch, imagine what it must feel like for your child to not be in full control of himself.

All this negativity makes it difficult for children with ADHD to feel optimistic and capable. We must discover, and help kids discover, what their strengths, interests, and passions are. This is what drives them, what motivates them. It is the key to helping them survive and thrive though the rest of what they *must* do — especially through school, where they often have little choice as to what they must focus on. It will be your job to balance the messages of negativity with support, optimism, and creativity. As you will see in the next chapter, sometimes you need to stack the deck in their favor to let them have a good day.

It's All in How You Frame It

There are some magnificently successful people who have fortunately allowed themselves to be identified publicly as people who have ADHD. I encourage you to read up on some of these people and how they feel ADHD impacted their lives and their successes.

- David Neeleman, founder of JetBlue Airlines
- Ty Pennington, host of *Extreme Makeover: Home Edition*
- James Carville, political consultant
- Sir Richard Branson, founder of Virgin Airlines
- Michael Phelps, Olympic gold medal swimmer
- Karina Smirnoff, dancer on *Dancing With the Stars*
- Adam Levine, Maroon 5 singer; coach on *The Voice*
- Shane Victorino, professional baseball player

Let these and others successful people be a source of comfort and inspiration to you and your child. ADHD is just a part of who your child is. And, in fact, it is often the very traits of ADHD that, when harnessed and mastered, can be a child's greatest strengths and assets.

Take a look at the left column below. This side represents many of the frustrating, negative traits often associated with having ADHD. Then look at the right side and see if you can visualize your child as that person—pretty awesome! You may want to mix up the order of the second column and ask your child to draw a line to match what he thinks could be a positive side of each trait on the left.

Hyperactive	→	Full of Energy
Strong-Willed	→	Tenacious, Persistent
Daydreamer	→	Creative, Imaginative
Daredevil	→	Risk Taker, Adventurous
Aggressive	→	Assertive
Slow Processor	→	Deep Thinker
Questions Authority	→	Independent Thinker
Lazy	→	Laid Back, Relaxed
Argumentative	→	Persuasive
Manipulative	→	Delegates Well
Bossy	→	Signs of Leadership
Distractible	→	Curious
Poor Sense of Time	→	Lives in the Moment
Difficulty Transitioning	→	Can Focus Intensely

Dr. Ned Hallowell, author of *Driven to Distraction*, says that people with ADHD have "magnificent minds"; in fact, they have "a Ferrari engine for a brain." The problem is that they have "bicycle brakes" and need to learn how to strengthen and control them—and that is where your knowledge, support, and guidance will come into play. Remind your child often of the positive side of his or her "magnificent brain."

Getting Your Black Belt

By now you are no doubt well aware of the complexities of parenting a child who has ADHD. This is not your typical parenting. Basic rules, structures, and reasoning do not always create the desired result. To complicate matters, as you will discover, when you are not aware of how to best respond to your child's erratic, frustrating, and challenging behaviors, you may inadvertently exacerbate the very behaviors you are trying to avert. Additionally, when as parents you are reluctant to pursue your parental expectations due to fear of your child's behavioral or emotional responses, you may unintentionally teach your child that his or her emotions can be used to manipulate others. Kids may learn that when they display negative emotions, they can get people to do what they want, which often is to leave them alone.

Dr. Russell Barkley (2010) put it this way:

> The arguing, defiance, refusal is a learned behavior—not genetic, not biological. It arises out of a pattern of behavior we have understood for 40 years. The way parents manage the emotional gambits of the child may make the emotions of the child better or worse and may teach the kid that emotions are a tool to use on others.

In fact, one study found that children of parents who reported a reluctance to engage in disciplinary actions because of fear of the child's behavioral response showed increasing rates of ODD symptoms in the following year (Burke, Pardini, & Lobber, 2008).

Your child may require more parenting than would be adequate for most kids. That is why you need a *black belt* in parenting! They need to rely on your strength. They need to feel that they have you to lean on and that you will be strong in the face of their chaos, stress, and anxiety. You must be calm, organized, consistent, and predictable for your child's sake. You need to be able to tolerate it when they may act as if (and express) that they hate you in the moment. Know in your heart, as they surely do, that you love them and will do what you think is necessary to be a good parent. Choose to be the parent you feel is best for your kid. What is our mantra? *Parent the child* you *have!*

Over the next seven chapters, we will methodically build a new home that will encompass each of the components needed for strong, supportive, and empathic parenting. Embrace my philosophy of *"Parent the child* you *have"* and you will gain confidence, skills, and strategies as you learn to trust your inner voice. Before you begin reading the next chapter, you may want to take a few days and just be a nonjudgmental observer of your child. Be curious. Next time your child doesn't come down when your call her for dinner, ask yourself, "Why?" Is she hyperfocused on what she's doing? Is she meaning to come but getting distracted? Is she unaware of how much time has passed since she said, "I'll be down in a minute?" Is she trying to avoid coming down for some reason but unable or afraid to share the real reason? The more you understand what motivates your child's behavior, the better you will be at helping her cope and adjust to her environment when possible and necessary.

This is where your journey begins . . .

Guiding Thoughts

1. Maintain a disability perspective.

   No one likes to think of their child as having a disability. However, the reality is that having ADHD, especially during the school years, can be a tremendous challenge. I find it valuable to acknowledge and accept that these challenges are real and impactful. We must *believe* the diagnosis—and then work to help strengthen our child, accept our child for who he or she is, and modify our expectations when necessary.

2. Stay in the present. Let your dreams for your child evolve as your child evolves.

It may take time for your child to mature and show his or her true capabilities—perhaps more time than for other kids. Remember that the development of *executive function* skills may be up to 30 percent delayed, so don't worry about comparing your child to other kids. Focus on the progress your child is making in his or her own life.

Homework

1. Be an observer of yourself and your child. Notice what you like and don't like in your interactions. Notice how much nonstructured time you have together and what goes on. Notice what behaviors seem related to some of the ADHD traits that were discussed in this chapter. Don't judge, don't worry about change; just notice.

2. Up until now you may have acted in ways, out of frustration or lack of understanding, that may not sit well with you. Write a letter to your child. You will not actually share this with your child; it is just for you. It is your opportunity to speak for yourself some of the unspoken thoughts and feelings you may be experiencing. Start with what makes you angry with your child, then add what makes you sad, then write down the fears you may have for your child and any regrets you may have. Finally, write about the love you feel for your child—the special thoughts you have that make you feel good. Get it all out—all the frustrations, all the annoyances. Then when you're ready, rip up the letter and let it go, and

begin to forgive yourself and your child. This is your time to begin your new path.

3. If you have not already done so, start a binder that will hold a running history of important papers regarding your child. It is difficult to anticipate what you may need in the years to come, but keep in mind that College Board that governs the SAT, LSAT, MCAT, and ACT Testing are independent corporations that make their own determinations regarding accommodations your child will be allowed to have when the time comes. You may need to show a historical record to support accommodations even if your school has approved them all along. Your child may end up wanting to become a lawyer or doctor and will need proof of need for law or medical board accommodations! I recommend including the following sections in your binder: doctors and professionals consulted (along with contact information); professional evaluations; medications, including name, dosage, duration of use, and impact; report cards; standardized testing; progress reports; school communications; IEP and/or 504 plans (for a basic description of these, please see Appendix B), and your yearly observations (milestones, concerns, successes). Always keep your original copies for your own records. What seems so clear now will sometimes become blurry in hindsight!

CREATE CALM

It *Really* Matters!

Leadership is a matter of having people look at you and gain confidence seeing how you react. If you are in control, they're in control.

—Tom Landry, Head Coach, Dallas Cowboys (1960–1988)

Do you ever find yourself, or perhaps your spouse, saying things such as, "If you would just calm down . . ." or, "I find myself yelling and getting so frustrated"? If you are like many parents I know, you may start the day promising, at least to yourself, that you will remain calm this time—but, somehow, something happens and the peace is broken. In the last chapter I asked you to take a few days and just notice how the broader description of ADHD and *executive function* skills development are impacting various aspects of your child's life and your interactions together. In this chapter, we are going to look at not only *why* calm matters, but also how to really pull it off!

What Role Does "Control" Play in Parenting?

As much as many kids may disagree, parents generally are not interested in just being in charge and giving their kids orders. Sure, it's nice to have things "our way" sometimes, but most parents I know are genuinely interested in living a happy, peaceful coexistence with their kids where laughter and joy prevail (with of course plenty of respect, learning, and hard work as well). Yet pretty early on, most parents find themselves having to give orders, set limits, and *control* much of the activity and decision making that goes on in the household. Why? Because we have to establish an environment complete with safety, learning opportunities, and some level of *order* to make sure certain essentials get done.

Some kids are like *clay*. They are flexible and adaptable. You can guide them with gentle, loving hands . . . to some extent. These kids are generally, though not always, reasonably compliant. They may object or complain from time to time, but they will mostly do what is asked of them, eventually.

Other kids are more like *cactus flowers*. They may be difficult to cultivate and may not be very flexible. They will not be rushed to bloom—they will open at their own rate. These are our strong-willed kids. They may be beautiful and sweet on the inside, but a bit difficult to handle. For these children, what may seem to be your benign attempts to simply direct them to eat, clean up, get ready, and do their schoolwork so that the world can move along smoothly are regarded as cause for challenge if not outright battle.

It is important for us as parents to strike the right balance between "control" and "controlling." When that balance does not exist, there is often fighting, chaos, and a whole lot of stress. It's exhausting, not to mention detrimental for all involved. As a parent, you do need to be in charge of the big picture, but knowing when and how to let go of some control is not so easy to discern. I think control in parenting refers to actively *deciding* when to take charge . . . and when to loosen the reigns. We will explore the when and the how later on, but for now we will see the impact control plays in our kids' lives.

A Quick Review of the Most Challenging Core Traits of ADHD

As we discussed in Chapter 1, there are many aspects of ADHD that can impact behavior and performance. And as the saying goes, "If you have met one person with ADHD, you have met one person with ADHD!" The traits will impact each child differently. In my practice, I have found these traits to create the greatest challenges for most kids with ADHD:

Deficits in emotional self-regulation
Slower processing speed
Weaker working memory
Difficulty regulating attention
Impulsivity
Poor sense of time
Executive function skills deficits

Always remember what it must feel like for these children every day—think of the chaos in their brains. I like the image of different colors of paint swirling together—beautiful, but chaotic at the same time.

Take a look at Figure 2.1. This used to be a fourth-grade math problem; however, with the new Common Core standards, it is apparently a third-grade problem! Try to imagine the balloon as representing the space in your child's brain for computing the answer to this problem. Every effort he or she expends to use each *executive function* puts pressure on the prefrontal cortex—the thinking part of the brain that houses the *executive function*. When you add in time pressure and performance expectations, for some kids it creates overload and the balloon bursts.

The math example is just one example. Your child may become overwhelmed by science or social studies or sports. Perhaps cleaning his room or doing art overwhelms him and causes him to shut down.

Our ability to process information, perform effectively, and regulate our emotions is impacted by what we are expected to manage. As Dr. Russell Barkley analogizes, we all have a limited fuel tank of energy available for controlling our emotions and responding to our world. However, for people with ADHD, because

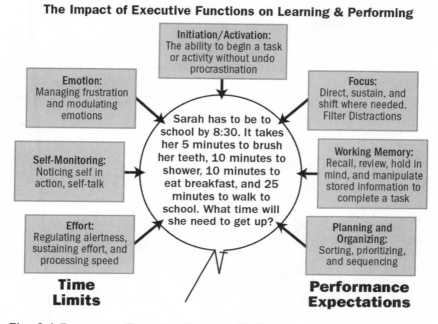

The Impact of Executive Functions on Learning & Performing

Initiation/Activation: The ability to begin a task or activity without undo procrastination

Emotion: Managing frustration and modulating emotions

Focus: Direct, sustain, and shift where needed. Filter Distractions

Self-Monitoring: Noticing self in action, self-talk

Sarah has to be to school by 8:30. It takes her 5 minutes to brush her teeth, 10 minutes to shower, 10 minutes to eat breakfast, and 25 minutes to walk to school. What time will she need to get up?

Working Memory: Recall, review, hold in mind, and manipulate stored information to complete a task

Effort: Regulating alertness, sustaining effort, and processing speed

Planning and Organizing: Sorting, prioritizing, and sequencing

Time Limits

Performance Expectations

Fig. 2.1 Pressure on Executive Function Skills

of their inherent deficits in emotional self-regulation, their fuel tank is more sensitive to the impact of their environment, expectations, and experiences. The more they are in a situation where they have to use *executive functions* that may be weak for the task, the more they deplete their self-regulation fuel to approach their world. Remember also that sleep, nutrition, and exercise quality can impact executive functioning and self-regulation skills as well.

It often takes kids with ADHD *so much more effort* to achieve what they do than their peers—from getting up and ready in the morning, to paying attention and keeping track of what they're doing, to dealing with the ebb and flow of their day. Try to visualize your child's body as a fuel tank, with her face being the fuel gauge. After a day of school, your child may not only be tired; she may also be dysregulated and much more prone to her ADHD symptoms. Her emotional self-regulation fuel tank may be on empty. If you tax her further before she has had an opportunity to refuel, you may experience conflict over even a minor request.

Tip: When your child comes home from school, realize that it may be no different than someone coming home from a hard day at work. No matter how anxious you are to hear about how her test went or know how much homework she has, she may have *no* interest in rehashing her day—especially if it was stressful or talking about it would create more stress. Offer a snack, perhaps some space, or some light conversation about your own day. Do what you can to help your child refuel.

Stress for our kids comes from many sources—our yelling, our fighting, and our pressuring them to meet our expectations. Then there is also academic, social, and extracurricular stress. For some people, certain levels of stress can be a motivator. In the short run it can actually get some people to comply, focus, work harder. Much of our well-intentioned yelling and pressuring is meant to motivate our kids to get off their butts and start working. Or it is meant to pressure them into complying with certain expected behaviors.

But guess what? Did you ever notice that all of this well-intended strategy of applying pressure might actually have the opposite effect?

We may have every reason in our minds to justify our anger, frustration, need to rush, and so forth, but I can assure you that in most cases, our stressful stance will have little positive impact on our kids. Likewise, if they are already in an agitated state, until they can genuinely feel calm, trusting, and safe, they will be unlikely to respond positively to the task before them.

Why?

Stress and pressure can shut down the *thinking* brain—the prefrontal cortex that houses *executive function* skills. Rational thought is overwhelmed and the brain goes into survival mode, where the emotional brain takes over. This part of the brain is called the *amygdala*. It is the primitive part of the brain that responds rapidly and reflexively. When you hear a sudden noise, the circuits connecting the thinking brain and the emotional brain shut down. The amygdala reacts immediately to potential danger. The thinking part of the brain disengages so that all of the body's resources can be devoted to survival. Many people get the feeling that they "just can't think straight" during moments of stress.

When the emotional brain is engaged due to a real or perceived threat, we sometimes go into *fight, flight,* or *freeze* mode. Keep in mind that kids with ADHD can be up to 30 percent delayed in their *executive function* skills that govern emotional regulation. Thus, the greater the pressure and stress are, the more their ability to concentrate, pay attention, and regulate their emotions may be compromised.

When kids lose their cool or don't do what we feel they need to be doing—or, worse, if they are doing things we feel they should *not* be doing—what feelings does this conjure up in most parents? Frustration, impatience, fear/anxiety, even anger? But what do our kids very often need most from us at these times? Someone who is calm, in control, safe to be with, and accepting of who they are and what they are experiencing. This is not easy—especially if you feel a clock ticking due to work needing to be done, meds that may be wearing off, different people's needs pulling at you, and your own emotional regulation skills!

So realize this:
Your wise lectures
Your pleading and bribing
Your reassurance
Your words of wisdom
Your threats of pending doom
. . . cannot be heard or properly processed.

Without calm, no learning can take place and
no problems can be solved.

CALM

Fig. 2.2 House: Calm

Building Our New Home

With each chapter, starting here, I am going to introduce an element to our new home. As with all homes, we must start with a solid foundation. That foundation for us is CALM (Figure 2.2).

There are four ingredients to the foundation of our Calm home.

1. Be the change you want to see in your child: Be CALM

For some of you, or perhaps your significant other, being calm is a tremendous challenge. Instead of focusing first on shaping and changing your child's behavior, you will need to focus instead on shaping and changing your own behavior. You must resolve to display and model self-control and self-regulation. For each person, the *how* we calm may be different; however, here are a few strategies that will be helpful to most people:

- Slow down and take a breath. A real, calming breath. Slow, deep, controlled breathing will actually change the chemistry in your brain and lower your blood pressure. Yoga is an excellent way to learn and practice relaxing breathing. In only one minute, you can experience a difference.
- Count to 10 slowly and rhythmically in your head. This is not the same as saying to your child, "I'm counting to ten and then you'd better . . ." This counting is meant for you—to slow yourself down and give you a chance to calm yourself.
- Lower and soften your voice. When speaking softly, it is a lot more difficult to express extreme emotion. It can change the whole mood.
- Notice your body language. You might try sitting down or putting your hands at your side, as this too makes it more difficult to appear agitated or threatening.
- Politely, without judgment, remove yourself from your child. It is very important that you be clear that you are not looking to reject or avoid your child, but rather that you need time to compose yourself so that you can respond more calmly and appropriately. The best thing to do is discuss, during a calm time, that this is something you might do as a way to help *you* calm down. In this way, you are beginning to model a helpful, appropriate calming technique for your child to copy.
- Remind yourself often that *without calm, no learning can take place*.

You are in charge of your *own* reaction! If it helps, post a sign in a few key places in your home that says *Calm is Power*. This will allow you to use *your* executive function skills so you can think, plan, and problem-solve.

2. Parent the child *you* have!

This philosophy will help you keep the proper perspective as you react and respond to your child.

- Let go of expectations connected to a timeline. Remember, your child may be up to 30 percent developmentally delayed—he may just need more time than his peers to show his true potential.
- Let your dreams for your child evolve as he evolves. He will surprise and delight you as he grows in ways you might not yet imagine.
- Slow things down and reduce certain expectations, at least for now. Doors don't always close forever if your child doesn't do everything *now*. Let go of the myth that your child will be missing out on his major opportunity if he doesn't start certain things now. History shows us many examples of magnificent late bloomers in life: Chef Julia Child didn't learn to cook until she was in her 40's; Grandma Moses started painting when she was 75 and ended up becoming one of the most famous American painters; and Col. Harland Sanders used his first Social Security check to launch the Kentucky Fried Chicken franchise when he was 65. For many people, just a few extra years to slow down and grow more is all they need to really start to flourish.
- Surround yourself with photos of your child that make you smile. Not those perfect portraits, but the candids that show him doing things, living life, and being happy.
- Let go of opinions and judgments from others who may not understand your true challenges and efforts. For those who understand, no explanations are necessary; for those who don't, sometimes no explanations are adequate.

3. Learn to express your feelings without shame, blame, or criticism

We will focus much more on communication in Chapter 4, but for now, try to notice the type of language you use when you need to correct or encourage your child. You catch more flies with honey than with vinegar—and you really will get more from your child when he or she can safely *hear* what you are saying. Replace the shame, blame, and criticism with *tolerance, empathy,* and *support.*

Once you begin to change your own behavior, control your anxiety, and become the calm rock in your home that your kids can count on, you will see this change sweep through your home. If you want your home to feel calm, it must start with you. Then you can begin to focus on how you and your child interact with one another.

4. Teach your kids how to be calm

There will be times when, for whatever reason, stress, anxiety, or anger disrupts a calm environment. While many kids can handle frustration, change, or disappointment relatively well, others have a *really* hard time. For some kids, it seems their level of calm can go from 0 to 100 in a split second. Be proactive in teaching your child *why* calm matters. A good place to start is by teaching them a few basic things about how their brain works. A short, simple lesson can help them understand, value, and take ownership of their actions. Of course, choose a calm, relaxed time to share this information. Don't worry if you are not ready to do this just yet; I will be giving you tools later on to help you *create* the time for these conversations.

Here are some basic things you can teach about the brain:

The front part of your brain, the thinking brain, is where your executive functions skills are. These are the areas that help you:

- *initiate actions/get started*
- *focus*
- *recall/use your memory*
- *plan and organize*
- *regulate your effort*
- *monitor how you are working*
- *manage your emotions*

You are the Chief Executive Officer of your brain. Think of each of the areas as a manager that is on your staff. It is your responsibility to train each part of your brain to function at its best. If one of your "managers" is struggling, I can help you learn tips, tools, and strategies to help you strengthen these skills and train the manager.

The back part of your brain has your amygdala. This is the part of your brain that manages emotions. When you are feeling extra stress, anxiety, or pressure, this emotional brain takes over and it is very difficult for your thinking brain to function at its best. Solving problems, learning, and performing become very difficult.

It may be helpful for you to also discuss the importance of the basic three elements of proper well-being: nutrition, exercise, and sleep. We each have unique needs in each of these areas, and helping your child be aware of his or her own requirements is a wonderful life lesson. When any of these elements is not at optimal personal levels, one's ability to handle daily responsibilities and stressors can be greatly compromised.

Tip: A word about sleep. Bodies truly do need enough sleep (which varies with age) to grow, repair, reduce stress, and learn. The American Academy of Pediatrics (AAP) states that children ages 3 to 10 should get between 10 and 12 hours of sleep each night; 11- and 12-year-olds should get 10 hours; and teenagers should get 9 hours of sleep. Especially as kids get older, we are finding that many are not getting the sleep they need. Teens tend to stay up especially late on account of homework, extracurricular activities, work, and screen time. Add to this the fact that their natural sleep cycle shifts as they mature, making it harder for them to fall asleep earlier. The AAP now supports a later school start time for teens, recognizing that research shows that their grades improve when they are allowed to get more sleep.

Even when your child is aware that being calm is important, it will not be easy for her to do so. Reminding her to calm down will not be sufficient if she does not have the skill or knowhow. You can help your child discover her best ways to calm down by exposing her to a variety of ideas and techniques. During a calm, stress-free time, brainstorm with your child ways she can help herself calm down and tools she can use to calm down so that she can be empowered to calm herself as she grows. Be open to providing her with the tools and the space she needs as she learns her own best ways. Here are some suggestions to get you started. More help will come in the next few chapters.

You can help your child recognize when she is "out of sorts" by gently naming what you see and helping her recognize her state of being (tired, hungry, frustrated, angry, bored, etc.). Rather than tell her how she feels, however, inquire or make a possible observation. "You seem . . . bored" or "I wonder if you are . . . hungry." Consider developing an "emotional thermometer" with your child (an example of one is provided in Figure 2.3).

This thermometer shows how the impact of the emotion "anger" can changes as one escalates from a calm state to a very agitated state. During a calm time, you can show this thermometer to your child, or better yet, help him create it with you as you ask him how he feels, how he acts, and what happens as a result of his reactions to hypothetical or past situations. You can create

Anger Thermometer

HOW YOU FEEL	HOW YOU ACT	CONSEQUENCE
Furious Enraged Boiling mad	Swear Curse Yell Become physical	Can't reason Angers others Possible punishment
Angry	Raise voice Say angry things	Not able to listen Trouble thinking
Upset Annoyed Frustrated	Calmly express feelings Look annoyed or upset	People listen Willing to compromise and reach solution
Calm	Happy Content	Productive Able to work with others

Without calm there is no learning!

Fig. 2.3 Emotion Thermometer

a similar thermometer to help him visualize the impact of stress, confidence, or any other emotion. Help your child recognize the warning signs in his thoughts or body that signals that he is getting upset. Also help him identify the things or situations that tend to trigger his negative moods. If he is frustrated or angry about something, teach him to immediately think of any three positive things he is grateful for to counter the negative thoughts. It won't make the other situation go away, but it might help him be in a better place to deal with it. Sometimes, a teacher may be willing to teach this thermometer to a whole class as a lesson. Kids are often more receptive to learning these things when they "have to" at school.

Make a plan or agreement with him as to how you will both handle things when he becomes upset. Sometimes your mere presence may escalate his intense emotions, and it may be better if you separate temporarily from him. It is important to communicate that you don't want him to feel rejected or abandoned if you decide that separating from him might be helpful. You are simply trying to give you both a chance to think.

Help your child avoid certain people or settings that he cannot manage—for now. If he feels anxious about going to a certain party or event, perhaps you can help him gracefully decline rather than pushing him to go. If going to Aunt Susan's house to play with cousin Sam usually doesn't go well, then perhaps it's best to skip these visits until better coping techniques are developed.

Proactively plan to modify a potentially triggering situation by discussing possible breaks, change of seating, and so forth. This might be helpful for outings such as religious or family events.

When possible, divert your child's attention away from triggering people or situations by mentioning or pointing out something off topic. Anything you can do to "break the current" of the intense emotion may work. A sense of humor might help, but be sensitive so that you do not appear unconcerned about your child's situation.

Have a special signal or code word you can use when your child has a play date or is in public to help him recognize that his emotions are escalating, and have a preplanned way to let him gracefully remove himself from the situation. Join your child for a snack and short game to break the tension. Have some games planned in advance that have a definite ending point and don't take very long (Connect Four, Master Mind, two hands of rummy, etc.). While this may seem as if you are rewarding him, you recognize that *without calm there is no learning* or problem solving, so it is best to return to calm so he can move forward. You can revisit the issue when cooler, calmer heads prevail.

Offer a hug and some empathetic words; solving the problem is sometimes secondary to the empathy he may need in the moment.

Depending on the age of your child, you may want to help him develop an *actual* or *virtual* "Calm Kit." An actual Calm Kit will have some physical items or representations of these items in the form of pictures or words. Your child can decorate a box or keep a backpack full of useful items. Keep a Calm Kit in your child's room, in the car, or in any other place where it might become useful. In creating an actual Calm Kit, you will certainly want to include your child. The process of making the kit may be a valuable lesson in and of itself. At times, merely having the physical kit will be enough to help your child call upon his or her reserves to switch gears and calm down. Be creative and change the contents often. Here are some physical items you may keep in the kit:

Stickers
Crayons
Paper
Bubbles (the act of blowing bubbles can help calm a child and regulate breathing)
Cards
Play-Doh
Small hand toys
Laminated card with ideas like I Spy and other interactive verbal games

You can discuss with your child the ways he can calm down that don't involve "things" that can be placed in a kit, such as the suggestions that follow:

- Have your child regulate his breathing and visualize his body relaxing.
    - ◊ *Try this:* At the beginning or end of a meal, or in the car, ask everyone to sit at the edge of their seat so that their backs are nice and straight and their feet are under their knees. Then have everyone breathe in through their nose slowly, then hold for 2 seconds, and then breathe out through their nose slowly. You can have everyone place one hand on their heart and one on their belly so they can feel their breathing. Repeat this three or four times each day. See if everyone can experience a nice, calm feeling.
- Make laminated cards with ideas your child has to help him calm down.
- Suggest quiet time in a room — just like a turtle learns to go into his shell when scared or threatened.
- Provide something for your child to use to vent his anger/frustration (drumsticks on a pillow, punching bag, etc.).
- Suggest physical exercise to release some tension. In fact, exercise increases levels of serotonin, norepinephrine, and dopamine in our brains. A lower level of serotonin is associated with depression. Try a brisk walk or run around the block, 5 minutes of basketball, "wall push-ups" (place your hands on the wall and lean in and out), handball, lifting weights. Playing ping-pong or Nerf ball against a wall can let you hit hard without causing any damage.
- Consider a bath or using some soothing scents.
- Provide a journal or pad of paper for your child to write down thoughts and feelings to help him gain clarity, release negativity, and perhaps begin to brainstorm a more positive response to the trigger.
- See if perhaps your child has or would like some type of soothing

blanket or cloth. It need not be associated with a baby blanket to bring true comfort and relaxation.

- Provide music or magazines to flip through.
- Help your child learn words of emotions ("I feel . . .") so he can tell you how he is feeling. For younger kids, you can print up Emoji pictures with different expressions and laminate them.

Once you have helped your child recapture calm, you can examine (in a nonjudgmental way) what caused the situation and make a plan to move forward. "Hey, what happened back there when I asked you to clear the table?" Try to reconnect with some gentle words or a hug. There will be more specific tools added in Key 5 for having these types of conversations.

Mindfulness

There is tremendous support for the notion that we can observe and respond to our thoughts and feelings in such a way that we can positively impact our state of mind. This is the essential core of mindfulness—the active process of noticing our thoughts and our feelings without judging them as good or bad and turning our attention away from distracting thoughts and toward a more positive, settling experience.

By teaching ourselves that instead of letting our thoughts and feelings control us, we can learn to live in the moment and reframe or refocus our attention, we can reduce our stress and anxiety and a more calm state can take over. A very simple way of teaching the concept of mindfulness to your child is to give him a piece of food (such as a chocolate candy or a bite of mashed potato) that he can hold in his mouth for a little while. Ask him to focus as much as he can on the sensations—the taste, the texture, the smell—for as long as he can. Afterward, help him to notice that during that time, other thoughts may not have been as present or powerful.

Learning and practicing mindfulness is a wonderful way to help manage stress and reduce the swing of emotional reactiveness so often associated with having ADHD. There is ample evidence to suggest that increases in attention, self-monitoring, and emotional processing occur for people who engage in meditation over an extended period of time.

Kids, as well as adults, can learn to use mindfulness techniques on a daily basis. I certainly would encourage you to learn the techniques and utilize them for yourself as well as introducing these concepts to your kid. Having this as a family or at least a joint venture between you and your child can have the added bonus of mutual support for learning and practicing. Besides, the old adage of "Do as I say and not as I do" has never been very successful!

For kids and young adults, you will want to make the practice shorter and perhaps more hands on. Excellent resources are listed in the homework section to help get you and your child started. As with starting any new exercise program, the key is to start with a commitment to scheduling time regularly for a few weeks until a new habit (and hopefully desire and appreciation) develops.

Final Thoughts on Calm

Let's start off with a basic truth: This is not easy. Especially if you, your partner, or your child is used to a form of coping and communicating that involves high levels of emotional reaction, making change is *hard*. But not only is change possible, it *is* effective and oh, so valuable! I have heard comment after comment from parents I work with telling me that the shift in themselves to stop justifying yelling and start calming down made drastic changes in the dynamics of their family life. Stress levels go down, problems can be handled, and loving feelings can grow. It may require you to modify some of your expectations and desires for now. It may also require you to increase your tolerance of your *child's* frustration levels when she is bored, disappointed, or angry. Sometimes you cannot, or *should* not, solve her problem—you can only help her cope with the feeling she is having. More support on helping your child do that is on the way.

So, as I said after the first chapter, give yourself a few days to digest and practice these concepts before moving on to the next chapter. I promise, there is no magic you will read in the end that will replace the steps you must take along the way.

Calm is your power!

Guiding Thoughts

- No learning can take place without calm.
- Stress and pressure can shut some kids down rather than motivate them.
- Sometimes it is our *own* stress that we need to manage. We may be very well intended when we rush our child, but the negative result is still the same. Saying to your child, "Laura, hurry up and finish your homework so you can join your friends in the park" may prompt Laura to become more stressed or frustrated that she can't rather than calm so that she can. Remember the diagnosis and the things that may be getting in the way of her ability to rush (slow processing speed, working memory deficits, focus, etc.) and realize that she may not be *able* to rush even if she wants to.
- We cannot control other people's behavior, but we can control our own. As much as we may attempt to encourage or restrict how another person acts, we can't—we can only respond afterward and work to anticipate beforehand. The only person we can really control is ourself. It is important for our kids also to learn that *they* are in control of their own reactions. Other people may annoy, disappoint, or hurt them, but they must not give those people power over their own reactions.

Homework

1. Discuss the importance and value of being able to calm down when necessary. Don't do this at a time when things are actively stressful or in a way that may seem punitive or judgmental. Review the suggestions listed in this chapter and begin to incorporate them into your day.

2. Make a "Top 5" list of calming strategies as a quick go-to source and place it somewhere in your personal field of vision for a daily reminder and support. I have heard it said that it takes 30 to 40 repetitions or two to three months to develop a new habit, so be patient with yourself and those around you!

3. Explore local resources for learning and practicing mindfulness and/ or meditation in person. Here are some books you can read:
    a. *8 Keys to Practicing Mindfulness* by Manuela Mischke-Reeds
    b. *The Mindful Child* by Susan Kaiser Greenland

KEY 3

STRENGTHEN CONNECTION

It's Their Survival Rope

"I was a success because you believed in me."
—Ulysses S. Grant in a letter to Abraham Lincoln

Remember when your kids were *just* cute and cuddly. Sometimes, especially if you are going through a particularly difficult time, it is hard to channel those thoughts. Hopefully you have several fond photos, memories and thoughts that are close enough for you to tap into even during the most frustrating of times.

For some of you, stress or chaos between you and your child may not be a big concern. For others, there may be an ever-present tension that you feel—how is the morning going to go? What will happen when she gets home from school? When will she to do her homework? How is the play date going to work out? Perhaps your child has a hard time just relaxing enough to be available to listen, learn, and adjust to new and different situations.

In the previous chapter I focused on understanding why calm matters (because *without calm, no learning can take place*!). I also gave a range of tools and strategies to help both parents and kids deal with those times when staying or returning to calm is difficult. Remember that change will take time, practice, and conscious effort—but the difference you see when you implement new strategies will be powerful.

What Is Your Objective in Being a Parent —and What Is Your Responsibility?

Most parents I work with are genuinely loving, caring people who want the very best for their kids. Some have gone to extraordinarily lengths to become parents; others had this greatness thrust upon them. Whatever your path, I ask you to take a moment to consider what you really hope to accomplish as parents. What traits do you want your kids to develop? When I discuss this issue in my workshops, I usually get responses that include traits such as *responsible, independent, successful, resilient, confident, respectful, self-aware,* and *self-disciplined.* There is one trait I always like to include as well—*emotionally connected.* Most parents want their kids to share a bond of love and warmth with them and with other members of the family. But where does happiness fit in? Who is responsible for their happiness? This is a more complex and important question than it may seem.

For instance, let's say your 7-year-old is disappointed that he can't go to the park because it started thundering and lightning. You offer suggestions of other things you can both do and plan another time to go to the park. Your son, however, starts crying and yelling, "It's not fair." Your attempts to engage him in other activities are met with anger and resistance. He is still arguing that he should get to play in the rain—a situation you have determined is unwise and unsafe.

It's not easy seeing your child sad. Should you keep trying to make him happy by offering more and more ideas? Should you compromise your gut and go outside just for a little so he hopefully sees it's not fun out there anyway (which of course could backfire as he discovers massive puddles for splashing in!). That depends on your goal—making him happy in the short term . . . or perhaps helping him learn that he *can* and in fact *is responsible* to deal with his disappointment and find a way to be happy.

Certainly, most parents want their kids to be happy. However, when parents feel responsible to make their kids happy, it has the ability to alter what their instincts may tell them to do in the moment.

Jonas Salk, inventor of the polio vaccine, once said, "Good parents give their kids roots and wings. Roots to know where home is and wings to fly away and exercise what has been taught them." Most parents would agree that they are responsible to provide their kids with at least a basic level of food, shelter, and clothing. More than that, I would include an obligation to provide an opportunity to learn, and an emotionally safe and, ideally, loving environment. But what about happiness? And what about guarding your kids from failure or disappointment? In the next few chapters, we will talk about ways to handle some of these important concerns, but for now, I ask you to consider how it feels to *not* be invested in their happiness and success—but rather in helping them develop their coping and regulating skills. It is said that true happiness is derived more from pride in accomplishments than from isolated experiences.

I know from having done this work for a while now that, while for some of you the relationship you have with your child is solid, for others who have been dealing with a "prickly cactus," it may be difficult to feel close in the moment—even though you know that inside your child lies a warm, sweet, beautiful person. You may have a child who is "high maintenance," requiring you to be actively parenting much of the time—correcting, prodding, redirecting, encouraging, soothing, and so forth. This can create a lot of wear and tear on your relationship.

All kids need strong bonds to grow up emotionally healthy. Kids with ADHD are wired differently. They have unique challenges that can sometimes make establishing these bonds more challenging—but no less important *and* rewarding. I talked earlier about how the world gives kids with ADHD so many negative messages about who they are and how they act. So often, at school and at home, much of the attention these kids receive is negative: "Stop tapping the pencil. Stop running around. Why can't you pay attention? Get started on your work already! Can't you think before you act?" On top of the negative messages many children receive from others, some of these kids pile on more negativity by comparing themselves to their peers—knowing, for instance, that they have the intelligence to do just as well in school but can't seem to show it in their performance. In addition to feeling down about themselves, they can begin to feel pessimistic about their futures.

All the negativity puts such a strain on them. And when they feel stress, it makes their symptoms worse. Remember how stress can shut down our *executive functions skills*, where impulse control, emotional regulation, reasoning, judgment, decision making,

Fig. 3.1 House: Connection

planning, and problem solving all happen? Some kids respond to the stress with aggression, others with avoidance. The thing is, just when some kids may be acting in the most challenging, frustrating ways, they need your stability, guidance, and warm nest even more. All kids crave connection with their parents—even when it seems as if they are repelling it. And yes, this goes for teens too! So just as the *foundation* of our home must be *calm*, the *core* of our home must be *connection* (Figure 3.1).

When interviewed on MSNBC's *Morning Joe* in 2014, Henry Winkler, actor and author of the *Hank Zipzer: The World's Greatest Underachiever* series (an excellent children's series about a boy with learning challenges) he advised parents, "A child knows they are not doing well, you don't need to remind them. All you need to do is keep that child buoyed. Because when you are not doing well your self image plummets to your ankles." For kids with ADHD, acceptance, encouragement, and positive attention are so crucial. We must build their armor—their belief in themselves and their future. We must help them have a positive internal voice by being their strongest external support. I once saw a greeting card that showed a photo of a kitten looking in a mirror and an image of a lion in the reflection. It said, "What matters most is how you see yourself."

Nothing is more powerful than the bond between parent and child. Without feeling truly accepted and unconditionally loved, it is very difficult to trust, to take risks, and to expose oneself. Your loving, emotional connection is the most powerful tool you can use to build your child's immunity to adverse life events, draw out her strengths, teach her life skills, and shape her behavior. It doesn't do the whole job, but without it the job never gets done right. A true, active connection—a strong bond with you—is your child's lifeline. You need to make your child's world feel safe so that she can take a chance on herself. Our kids need to know *we believe in them* and will never stop trying to find ways to help them and understand them. You have the opportunity to truly discover the depths of your own love. It can be transformational.

Creating a Deep, Lasting Connection

It starts, of course, with *"Parent the child you have."* It is some-times helpful to remind yourself that ADHD is a neurological disorder. For now, your child is not always able to monitor his own behavior. We will work on helping him modify his behavior a little later on, but for now you need to work on your foundation of building a strong connection so that he can trust and grow as he needs. As a parent, you need to understand how your child thinks, what challenges he faces, and what motivates him. You also need to help *him* understand for himself how his own brain works so that together you can be prepared to face his challenges armed with tools, strategies, and the hopeful perspective that he *can* and *will* achieve. As I mentioned in Key 2, it is often helpful to explain to kids the basics of how their brain works and what happens to their ability to solve problems when they are stressed or anxious.

Listen to the Song Your Child Is Trying to Sing

Each child is born with innate gifts, talents, and passions. Some-times your child's interests are not what you would expect—or in truth, desire. And sometimes it may seem that she floats from one thing to the next so frequently that it's hard to tell *what* she is really interested in. Be patient—these years are for exploration. Very rarely does someone stay with one interest or profession that he or she chose so early on. And if you do have one of those rare kids who is so single-minded, her drive will keep her on track more than your prodding. For now, helping her feel good about who she is and knowing that you are in her corner is more valuable than the activities she chooses to focus on.

Often, parents are guided to start making changes in their kids by focusing on reducing negative behaviors. This will be much more easily accomplished when we start, instead, with building on what *is* working. With all the negative feedback our children receive from themselves and others, we want to create a balance for our kids. We can start doing that by drastically increasing the positive feedback they receive. Remember, your greatest role as a parent is to form a strong connection with your child to help support him in him growth.

How do we cement that connection with our kids? By providing positive recognition for who they are and what they do. How? By catching them in the act of being good—even if we have to create the opportunity!

Actively paying attention to our kids' good behavior is not something we always do. We may see them doing something good; we may think about it; it may even make us smile. But do we always let them know they have done something good? Sometimes. But often, parents take this opportunity to do some chores, read a magazine, or make a phone call. After all, why interrupt a good thing? The answer is simple—because positive reinforcement and praise not only build a kid's self-esteem but also serve to strengthen the bond between you and your child. Kids notice when you have more time for them when they are acting out than when they are playing peacefully. The dishes may seem important to do when they are playing nicely, but suddenly they are not as important when you hear fighting going on. Be careful not to have time for them only when they are in need of correction. It's about the relationship, not just giving them attention.

Encouragement—Not Just Simple Praise

Praise has the ability to build self-esteem, autonomy, self-reliance, self-awareness, and motivation for learning more. But praise can also be viewed as manipulative. While very young children are likely to take praise at face value, older children may become suspicious if it does not feel true and heart felt. Tell a child he is doing "great" when he has perhaps become more self-aware and is cognizant of others' performance, and he may not accept your comment as genuine. Praise can also unintentionally reduce a child's motivation and optimism in his ability to learn and succeed, as I will show shortly.

For praise to be effective in helping your child learn and grow, it must focus on specific feedback about his effort and intent, not just the outcome. Remember how I said in Key 1 that kids with ADHD have lower levels of dopamine, causing an understimulation in the reward and motivation centers in the brain? Some kids aren't as motivated by pleasing others, so praise in itself may not be a motivator unless it provides feedback they find useful.

Praise also can have a powerful impact on a child's *"mindset"* for learning. Carol Dweck, a researcher in the field of motivation, found that the words we use in commenting on kids' work can greatly affect their motivation and effort in learning. During a research study on typical seventh-grade students, she administered a series of puzzles that were easy enough for all the children to do fairly well. She randomly divided the group. Half of the students were praised for their *intelligence* and told, "You must be smart at this." The other students were praised for their *effort* and told, "You must have worked really hard." The results were very clear. Those who had been praised for their effort welcomed more challenging puzzles and spent more time working on them, while those who had been praised for their intelligence became reluctant to tackle more challenging puzzles for fear of not looking smart and of risking embarrassment. In subsequent tests, they did more poorly than their peers who had been praised for their effort, ostensibly because they did not believe *their* effort was the crucial variable, so they did not work as hard or as long. She found that when we praise kids for their intelligence, looking intelligent becomes the focus, so they do not take risks that may lead to mistakes.

If we want to help our kids develop a *"growth mindset,"* one where they believe that their intelligence and expertise can be developed through their effort and learning, then we must be careful to comment on their *process* more than their *result*. Their effort in many cases is far more important than the outcome. It is steps on the pathway, forward movement.

Effective and Impactful Praise

When you praise your kids, be careful not to pair your praise with judgment or evaluation, such as, "You are the *best* artist." Such emphasis on competition or comparison may evoke disbelief or pressure to perform. It is also important to draw the distinction between their pleasing you and their doing a good thing. When you say, "I am proud of you," it is about how they made you feel. They may derive pleasure for making you feel good; however, we can do much more with our words than that! When you can identify and label the specific qualities you respect, not their actions or accomplishments, you are giving them valuable feedback. What they do is received, registered, and reflected back so everyone involved notes what happened. It helps them make the internal connection between what they do and feeling good. They see these qualities for themselves and take pride in what they have done. Your goal is to help build their self-confidence while showing them that you respect them and the choices they are making in that moment. Acting well and doing well are coupled with a loving, warm feeling from you. You want their feeling of pride to come from within, not just in knowing that they are pleasing you.

The Formula for Effective Praise: The 3 Ns

Focus on these three steps:

1. *Notice* your child doing something positive
2. *Name* what you have noticed and the value you see in it
3. *Nourish* your kid with warmth—a brief comment or nonverbal reaction

Which would you rather hear?

"Nice outfit."

or

"Sally, I see you put a lot of thought into the outfit you put together. I see the pride you take in how you appear and the care you put into something that is important to you. I really respect that about you."

Now, you need not be *that* effusive each time; however, I hope this demonstrates how wonderfully impactful your words can be!

Here are a few more examples:

- "I see you've been rearranging those blocks to get them to look a certain way for you. You look like you are really concentrating hard."
- "You've tried a few different ways to mix the color you want to create. I see you are very patient."
- "I notice that your brother ruined the picture you were working on. I see you managed your anger and used your words to tell him how you felt. Good job."
- "I know you were excited to tell me what happened in the game you were playing. I appreciate that you waited patiently until I got off the phone."
- "Joshua, I see that memorizing the Spanish vocabulary words is difficult for you. You are working very hard, and I see that you are not giving up. Nice effort!"

Nonverbal feedback can often be an effective tool as well:

- A hug
- A smile
- An affectionate rub on the head or shoulder
- A wink
- An arm around the shoulder
- A gentle kiss

Sometimes a little practice can help make the words roll off your tongue more easily. Try seeing what you might say to provide encouragement in these situations:

- You see your child and a friend playing with blocks together and everything seems to be going okay.
- Your child, who previously would not start her homework without much prodding, went to work on it when the timer to begin went off.
- You overhear your son encouraging another boy to try to hit the ball.
- Your daughter helps you fold the laundry, although she doesn't do it quite right.

Remember, your goal is to break the pattern of negativity that your child experiences. This does not mean that you cannot or should not correct negative behavior. As we will explore during the next chapter, it's *how* you say it that matters! Research has shown that in families where there is a high incidence of non-compliance, meaning that kids are not cooperative or even defiant, there is less active positive recognition and encouragement of good behavior from parents—even when the good behavior exists. A helpful way to begin to rebalance the attention you pay to your child is with a penny count: Put 10 pennies in each pocket at the beginning of the day. Each time you must correct your child, transfer a penny to the left pocket. Each time you praise your child, transfer a penny to the right pocket. Count the pennies in each pocket at the end of the day and commit to increasing the positive comments each day.

Your child, especially if you have an adolescent or older child, may notice that you are speaking differently. This may seem odd, annoying, or off-putting at first. Explain the truth: "I realize I have been focusing on the negative and stressful actions, and that I wasn't paying enough attention to the good things that you do. I am working to correct this. I love you and care about you. I truly believe in you and your ability to do well, and I want to make sure you realize how I feel."

Building Connection

Deepening your connection and bond with your child takes time. I suggest that you actively plan to spend one-on-one time with your child. Aim to spend 20 to 30 minutes with your child three times each week for the next three weeks. This may seem unreachable—only you know what is really possible. Just keep in mind that there cannot be enough *quality time* without spending *quantity time*. So get ready to spend some terrific time with your child, whom you love and want to nourish. Don't worry about shaping and changing your child's behavior during this special time; think instead about shaping and changing your relationship together. It's so vital for you both to have these positive experiences to fall back on when things become strained or stressful. Actively spending joyful time to break some of the stress also gives you the chance to accentuate the positive. Celebrate who your child is, ADHD and all—his energy, creativity, uniqueness, and so forth. Spending one-on-one time with your child creates an opportunity for you to:

- Get to know your child in deeper and richer ways than you may have known him or her before
- Deepen your connection with your child—to build trust and love and create wonderful opportunities to learn about each other
- Learn more about your child's interests, fears, concerns, styles, and motivations
- Catch your child in the act of doing positive things that you can comment about. Remember: *Notice, Name,* and *Nourish!*

We all need to feel special and valued. What better way to say to your child, "I love you and love just being with you" than to tell him or her, "Let's make sure we put aside special time for us together!" After all, play is really kids' main way of communicating. That's when all the good stuff comes out. It certainly doesn't come out after school. "How was your day? " "Fine" "What did you learn?" "Nothing." It's usually not until bedtime when you really get to hear about the fight they had or the problem with the teacher! In fact, I strongly recommend that for the first 10 minutes after they come home from school, you don't even ask them specifics about the day. Certainly if they initiate it, go with their direction. But be aware that they may need a break from the stress of their day and a chance to unwind a bit (and refuel), just as grown-ups do.

Just follow these guidelines for your one-on-one time together and enjoy!

- Tell your child that you would like to spend special "one-on-one" time with her. Let her know when and how long you are planning to spend with her. No, this doesn't mean you won't spend other time with her—this is just a special time that you both get to look forward to together. For older children and teens of course you will choose a time together.
- No other children can be involved in this time—this is your special time with one child. If you have more than one child, plan separate time for each one.
- Let your child choose what you will do together. This is a great time to help her explore her interests. Try to avoid TV, as it is primarily a passive activity, but video games that are interactive are acceptable. If your feel it might be helpful, give your child a few choices of activities you think will appeal to her.
- Refrain from giving directions, making corrections, or giving instruction during the activity. Ask questions if you are curious, but not to direct the activity. You want this activity to be time led by your child.
- This should be nonjudgmental, nonteaching time. Make only positive, neutral, or descriptive comments. (This is easier said than done.)
- Ignore minor misbehaviors. Determine within yourself whether the behavior is merely irritating or more serious. If it is minor,

briefly ignore it until the behavior stops. Then make a positive comment. If it is more serious, then stop the exercise and correct the behavior. If you need to end the time together completely, let your child know that you will spend one-on-one time with her again tomorrow (or whenever you have determined) and that the next time will go better.

- Relax and enjoy—there is nothing that needs to be accomplished other than a positive experience with your child. Show interest in what your child is interested in.
- Be patient and forgiving with yourself if it doesn't go perfectly the first few times. Just stay with it and adjust what you need to.

A Note About the Teen Years

With teens, you may get some resistance when you try to plan one-on-one time. Some parents complain that their teens won't talk to them and don't want them in their lives. This is the development stage they are in—seeking to separate from you so they can see themselves as individuals. In fact, what does a teenager say when a parent says "white"? They say "black"! This *is* a very challenging time for parents!

As children become teenagers and are able to be more independent, that doesn't mean they don't still need (and secretly want) their parents in their lives—it just takes more effort, patience, and a bit of psychology to create shared time. When our kids are young, we are their closest companions, involved in many aspects of their lives. I think that sometimes the shift is harder for parents, as they must redefine their own role and start accepting that the child they have is developing his or her *own unique tastes, interests, styles, and dreams.* While this is cute and inspiring when children are young, as they become teens you see that there are greater ramifications to their differing desires and choices. Letting go is not easy. It is further exacerbated by the reality that often teens are wanting freedoms and responsibilities that they have not yet demonstrated they can handle—especially kids with ADHD, whose *executive function* skills are developmentally delayed!

Start where you are and build from there. We will have a much better opportunity to help them through this period if we accept that it really is their *job* to challenge and find their unique way. Our *job* as parents is to stay connected through the process. Talk less, listen more—but spend time together! Keep in mind that it's not emancipation they seek—it's independence. Sometimes they just want to share to stay connected but don't really want your input or involvement. If you are unsure whether they are seeking your advice or just wanting to share, ask them—believe me, they will tell you and will appreciate your interest and your acceptance of the space they may be seeking.

The value of listening is twofold—you get to hear what's on their mind and heart and, equally important at times, they get to hear themselves. They get to articulate their thoughts, concerns, fears, questions, ideas, and so forth in a way they may not have in their own conversations with themselves.

If your child is reluctant to spend time with you or communicate with you, either because of a strained relationship or because of typical teen resistance, try texting or writing a simple note: "Hey, let's plan some time together . . . you choose the activity and time." Ask him to give it a chance, letting him know that you miss stress-free time with him and have no hidden agenda. If you still have trouble planning time, ask if you can join him in an activity he's doing alone—even if it's watching TV or playing a computer game. Or wait until your teen is doing something he enjoys and make some positive observations; see if you can hang around a few minutes. Perhaps offer to make breakfast or a snack just to spend time with him. Consider texting with him; it's a great way to calmly communicate and allow him the control he may seek in terms of exposing himself to you.

Other Ways to Build Connection

- Routines, rituals, and traditions have a wonderful way of bringing people together. Whether it is a religious event or a Sunday night dinner, the regularity of the gathering allows for guaranteed time spent together. Infusing this time with unique family traditions can create special memories and bonds.

- Framing photos, and telling stories about past events connected to the photos, can remind kids and parents of joyful times spent together. It's the candid, random photos more than the perfectly posed ones that evoke the emotional connection to the heart. Kids may forget some of the fun times spent together, so feel free to say, "Remember when . . ." to help them "create" the memory. These days, many people post pictures of past events on their social media account for "Throwback Thursday." Your child may not appreciate being embarrassed publicly, but perhaps you can text them an old photo privately every couple of weeks.

- Create a secret family signal. Whether it's a tug on the ear (as entertainer Carol Burnett used to do as she signed off her TV show each week) or a pat on your own heart, it's a great way to discreetly tell your child you love him without embarrassing him in public or when the distance is too far or the situation is not conducive to communicating verbally (such as when they are on stage performing or on the bus headed to school).

- Take interest in something *they* like, even if it is not something you really enjoy. Learn the characters in their favorite video game or let them teach you how to master the next level. Kids feel great when they can teach *you* something for a change.

- Ask your child to think of ten words that describe him. Then ask him to choose the five he is most proud of. If he struggles, offer some of your own insights. We may often say, "I love you," but let him know why you *like* him.

- Find a picture of your child that makes you smile and frame it with the saying "Praise every day." The world can assume you are "praising the day" when you had your child, but you will know you it's your reminder to praise (encourage) him every day!

Whether we realize it or not, our kids are always watching us. They read our expectations of them, although not always accurately. You may be deep in your own thoughts about whether you should try out a new recipe for dinner. As you unconsciously shake your head no, your child may assume you have just disapproved of something she has done. What is she reading on your face? Notice your voice and your posture, not just the words you use with them. As novelist Toni Morrison said, "Let your face light up when your kid enters your space." Look up from the dishes and take a moment to smile and say hello—and mean it. It only takes a moment to connect.

Guiding Thoughts

- Being connected gives you the best opportunity to teach your child and help your child shape his or her behavior.
- There cannot be enough *quality time* without spending *quantity time*.
- Negative feedback may stop behavior, but positive feedback can help improve behavior.
- Praise with impact: Notice, Name and Nurture.

I've learned that people will forget what you said, people will forget what you did, but people will never forget how you made them feel.

—Maya Angelou (1928–2014)

Homework

1. Plan one-on-one time with your child using the guidelines outlined in this chapter.
2. Find one special photo of your child that makes you smile and put it in a place you will see each day as a reminder of your goal to praise him or her often.

KEY 4

CULTIVATE GOOD COMMUNICATION

The Road to Cooperation, Compliance, and Positive Action

Courage is what it takes to stand up and speak; courage is also what it takes to sit down and listen.

—Winston Churchill

I have addressed the value of having a strong, connected relationship with your child, so that you can be in his life to teach him, support him, and balance some of the negative messages he receives from himself and the outside world. Not to mention, the enjoyment of being with this child you are sharing your life with. I hope you are starting to share more *kid-centered, non-agenda* time together and that you have been working on bringing more awareness to creating calm in your home.

Often, parents express that even though their relationship with their children is okay, they still have a difficult time getting their kids to *do* what they are asked to do, *speak* in a respectful manner, or *behave* appropriately in a range of situations. I am going to talk now about *defiance* in a broad context. Webster's dictionary defines defiance as "a refusal to obey something or someone." Defiance is not always loud, active resistance. Sometimes defiance is simply avoidance, postponement, or deflection. Before we can tackle how to *decrease* some of the defiance as well as the stress and chaos that comes with it, we need to take a closer look at what role we, as parents, play as well as why kids are *really* defying in the first place.

The Defiance Dance

At a basic level, when you make a request of your child (e.g., to take out the garbage or start working on homework), either she is going to do it now or she is not. If she complies, we have an *endpoint*—represented in Figure 4.1 by a smiling Emoji. If she does not, she has either *ignored* your request, *postponed* doing what was requested ("I'll be down in a minute"), or *refused* outright ("I will not"). You now have an *"unmet expectation."* We will explore shortly the reasons why a child may not do as we have requested, but for now I am going to call each of these three possible reactions "defiance." You really have four options for response:

The Defiance Dance

They will not change their dance steps until you change yours.

Fig. 4.1 The Defiance Dance

1. *Repeat* your request. Do you ever find yourself continually calling out the same request, hoping that eventually your child will comply? At some point, for whatever reason, your child may meet your expectation—but there is no guarantee how many times you will need to repeat your request before it is met. At some point, you may get frustrated and switch your dance steps to one of the other three options. *The dance continues . . .*

2. *Give up* on your request. "Fine, I'll get the ketchup!" Sometimes, as we will explore later, parents decide for whatever reason to let go of their expectation, perhaps leaving the child with the impression that her response (or lack thereof) influenced her mom's or dad's change of heart. You have at least reached an *endpoint* in your dance.

3. *Threaten* some action. When you threaten your child with potential consequences, it often sounds like, "If you don't . . . then I will . . ." If your child senses that this is not an actual plan but rather just a threat or a possibility, she may hold out until your word is weakened or you somehow realize that you will not carry through with your threat. I once had a parent tell me that she told her 9-year-old son she would cancel his play date if he didn't go brush his teeth. Having no history of follow-through in the past, the child knew this was likely an empty threat and continued playing until he was done. *The dance continues . . .*

4. *Assert your control* (punish the refusal; restrict use of an object or some other freedom). "That's it; you may not play with your computer for one week." You may be a parent who follows through on your word, and often this can be an effective way of managing a situation in the moment. Many parents report, however, that they are constantly having to punish or restrict their child and that it seems to have no positive effect on *changing* or *preventing* certain behaviors. And, they find that situations or conditions escalate to the point that they feel they have run out of impactful punishments. For now, at least, you have reached an *endpoint* in your dance.

Each of these responses may have a very appropriate place in your parenting. The vital part here, which we will explore very shortly, is how each of these "moves" is communicated and carried out. As you can see in the diagram, when you *repeat* or *threaten*, the same dance steps will appear, with no end in sight. The fact is, *they will not change their dance steps* until *you change yours!* Their defiance allows them to continue doing what they want, or avoid doing what they don't want.

Conventional Parenting Wisdom

Many adults believe that kids, especially kids with ADHD who exhibit inconsistent, off-task, and difficult behavior, will do the right thing "if they *want* to." "If she wants to do well on the test, she will study." "If he wanted to keep his room clean, he would." "If he wanted to get along better with his sister, he would try harder." The assumption is that defiant behavior is used to gain attention or to manipulate or coerce others into giving in to the child's wishes. Conventional wisdom is that kids want *power* and *control* over their lives—and are willing to fight for it. They believe the problem is that kids are not always intrinsically motivated to do what they must to cooperate and succeed. Based on that philosophy, parents' role is to . . . make kids *want* to. And how do parents often go about making kids "want to"? *Rewards and punishments.*

Your Explanation Guides Your Intervention

We have probably all done this at one time or another—seen your child sitting around playing, watching TV, talking on the phone, or some other "nonessential" activity. It's 4:30 in the afternoon on a school day and a thought—no, an assumption—wells up inside that says, "Hmm, he should be doing his homework." You have faced this situation before and this little voice, which is growing louder by the moment, is telling you that you'd better intervene. So you approach your son and say, "Why aren't you doing your homework?" Now, if you look at the mother's stance and expression in Figure 4.2, you can probably guess the tone and attitude with which she asks her son the question.

Lest you think the boy's response is far-fetched, I will tell you that in my professional work, I have come across this type of response on more than one occasion. In fact, I once coached a teen who had a very interesting approach to managing his wishes. This boy (we will call him Henry) was in tenth grade and had previously been an excellent student. His parents contacted me at one point, however, because his grades had steadily declined and his efforts to do work had all but stopped. The dad's "explanation" was that since Henry had ADHD, perhaps he just needed more support knowing *how* to organize, manage his time, and get himself started. He felt that Henry wasn't really trying his best to learn, and needed a push. His "intervention" was based on the idea that Henry just needed the right motivation (rewards or punishments) and some outside support in order to get back on track. Henry's parents tried many of the typical approaches: increasing the monitoring of his homework, tighter communication with his teach-

"IF I DO MY HOMEWORK, I'LL GET GOOD GRADES.
IF I GET GOOD GRADES, YOU'LL SEND ME TO COLLEGE.
IF I GO TO COLLEGE, I'LL GRADUATE AND GET A JOB.
IF I GET A JOB, I MIGHT GET FIRED. IF I GET FIRED,
I COULD GO BANKRUPT AND LOSE EVERYTHING.
THAT'S WHY I DIDN'T DO MY HOMEWORK!"

Fig. 4.2 Why aren't you doing your Homework? © *Randy Glasbergen/glasbergen.com*

ers, offering to reward him for completing his work and improving his grades, and finally threatening and punishing Henry when he did not improve on his efforts.

As I got to know Henry, it became clear to me that a power struggle had developed between Henry and his parents, in particular his dad. You see, Henry's dad was a lawyer. His grandfather was a lawyer. And . . . you guessed it, Henry was being groomed to go to law school and become a lawyer. At this time in Henry's life, he wanted nothing to do with wearing a suit and tie like his dad, working in an office, and being a lawyer. He did, however, have a serious interest in rap music—specifically, he wanted to manage and promote rap musicians.

Henry's father, unfortunately, despised rap music, did not take his son's interest seriously, and felt it important only that Henry get good grades to keep his options for his future open. Clearly he had not read my philosophy that allowing our kids to explore and pursue their interests is not just about developing their long-term talents and goals, but often more about exploring and developing their sense of themselves, and in having experiences that teach them about how the real world operates.

By belittling and stifling Henry's interest in exploring rap music, Henry's dad succeeded in helping him develop his new academic plan. "If I don't do my homework, I won't get good grades. If I don't get good grades, you can't send me to college. If I don't go to college, I can't go to law school. Then I won't have to wear a suit and tie and I can become what I want to become— a rap music manager!"

The *intervention* that was really needed to help Henry was to help him and his dad develop a relationship—a true connection to start the necessary repair work.

How We Speak to Our Kids

How we communicate our expectations, concerns, and requests has a profound ability to trigger our children. In Figure 4.2, there could be *several* explanations as to why the boy was watching TV at 4:30 p.m. Sure, perhaps he wasn't doing his homework and may not have intended to complete it. But there are other possibilities as well: Maybe he had no homework. Maybe he had planned out when to do it and was on target with his plan. Maybe his homework *was* to watch a particular television program! The point is, just by the stance the mom took and the voice she spoke with, she communicated that she already *assumed* that her son was wrong, bad, and a disappointment to his mother. In such a scenario, we have already set up an *offense/defense* confrontation. A child—or adult—is likely to either shut down or snap back when put in this position. As the adult, we need to be careful not to instigate a negative discourse or engage or continue in a power struggle.

If you have ever watched kids choosing teams for a baseball game, you may have seen the two captains taking turns placing their hands on the baseball bat—starting at the fat tip and working their way up to the butt. Whoever's hand is last on top wins the first choice of players for his team. In our case, think of you and your child as putting your hands up the bat—but the bat goes on forever, and every time you put your hand higher, so does your child! This bat represents the *power struggle*. Have you ever gotten into a "yes"/"no" battle with a child? Does the child ever stop and say, "Okay, you win"? It is generally best if *we adults* stop the escalation and "drop the bat." This doesn't mean we give in; it means we change the course and nature of the conversation. We need to find an *endpoint*—and sometimes may even need to create a *calm* intervention before we do so.

We know that "defiance" is "a refusal to obey something or someone." I believe that defiance is also a *learned behavior* and *a coping technique*—not a good or effective one, but a technique nonetheless. It allows kids to continue doing what they want to do, or avoiding what they don't want to do or believe that they *can't* do! If a child learns from experience that by refusing to comply, she can actually manipulate others in her world to somehow back off or compensate her, she learns that she can affect the outcome of situations by defying. But does this really "work" for her? It may get her out of doing certain things, but I would argue that she is not walking around happy and satisfied with herself.

Why Do Kids Defy in the First Place?

Often, it would seem that the easier, more pleasant path would be one where kids just stop the battling and do what they are asked. As parents, our gut often tells us that "if they would just . . . [study for 15 minutes, do their homework right after school, pack up their stuff the night before, go to sleep earlier, come to dinner when they are called, not wait until the last minute, etc.], things would be so much easier for them." And yet, this logic and reasoning seems to escape them. Or does it? Some people believe the acting out is intended to seek attention or to gain power or control over others. This does not seem to be the reason in most cases. When you scratch the surface of a noncompliant or challenging child, you may discover a myriad of reasons driving their behavior. We have to truly delve into their experience of the world and understand our child. Here are some of the reasons kids may spend their energy resisting "just doing what they should":

- They are trying to deflect the expectation to protect their self-image. Saying, "math is stupid" or "I don't care about how I write" is easier to say and feel than "I can't," "I don't know how," or "I feel dumb."
- They don't know how to do what is expected. It only takes a second for a child with ADHD to get distracted, lose his place, and then have no idea what is going on. Add to that his slower processing speed, so that when he checks back in it takes him longer to pick up and catch up to everyone else. Often, if a child asks the teacher to retell or re-explain, he is berated for not listening. And if he asks another student, he gets in trouble for talking in class. Either way, he is shamed.
- They are hyperfocused—they really *didn't* hear. But they really

didn't! People with ADHD can be so tuned in to what they are doing that the outside world seems to disappear.

- They are asserting independence. For some kids—and you know if you have one of them—following their *own* instincts and path is more important to them then succeeding through the help of others. And while this may seem exasperating and frustrating, especially when they seem to jeopardize more opportunities than they create, I believe their inner will to succeed and shape who they are is to be somehow encouraged, embraced, and acknowledged. Not that they should not be held accountable to others for their responsibilities, but they are not stallions to be broken—rather, saplings to be nurtured and supported.

- They have been given unreasonable or unrealistic expectations. Remember, *"parent the child you have."* There are things that for a whole host of reasons your child should not and cannot be expected to do on par with his or her peers—at least for now and at least under the same conditions. Think about some of the conditions that make learning and performing challenging: working memory deficits, poor sense of time, slower processing speed, difficulty regulating emotional responses, sustaining focus and effort, and so on. *Remember the diagnosis!*

- They don't feel connected or trust that they will be *heard.* I think it's human nature to resist performing at our best for others whom we don't trust, admire, respect, or appreciate. Think about Henry—he so resented his father's view of him and his interests that the last thing he wanted to do was please his father, even at the expense of his own success!

- They receive differing expectations and kudos from Mom and Dad. Even the best of couples have different dreams and hopes for their kids. But when one parent seems to value something that the other parent does not, it can sometimes put the child in a very difficult situation. "Do I go to hockey practice or study for my exam?" I cannot stress enough how important it is that parents work out their differences *in advance and in private* before putting their kids in a position where they have to choose who to please and who to disappoint, or worse.

- There are inconsistent rules, expectations, and consequences. "Mom didn't seem to care last time when I didn't do my homework." "Dad said I could stay out late last time; why is this time different?" If they don't know when you will really care, why not do as they please until it matters? Remember the dance steps where you either keep *requesting* or *threatening*.

- The parenting style is excessively controlling. Some parents, out of anxiety, philosophy, or lack of awareness, establish rules and expectations that may be out of step with societal norms or developmental stages. This can place a heavy burden and stress on children as they try to balance respecting their parents with growing and developing as they are perhaps intended. Parental anxiety may be brought about by a loving fear that a child may not succeed or may experience emotional hurt. However, by holding a child back, other problems may also surface as the child fights for freedom and opportunity. And when kids are far out of step with their peers in terms of freedoms and expectations, this can cause some to battle for their independence even more than is typically seen at their age.

These are kids in desperate need of your guidance, acceptance, love, and support. Yet the way they approach their lives and those around them often conjures up feelings of anger, resentment, frustration, and disapproval in the ones who love them the most. So remember—*your explanation guides your intervention.* Next time your child is not doing as she "should," rather than just looking at her behavior, ask yourself what might be *behind the defiance.*

Breaking the Cycle of Defiance

Generally, kids will learn to change their behavior not just because others around them don't approve of their behavior, but rather because they recognize how it will benefit them. By being aware of your child's underlying insecurities and vulnerabilities, and in

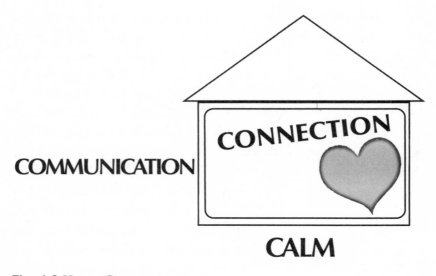

Fig. 4.3 House: Communication

forming a strong connection with her, you can help her gain the confidence and skills she needs to develop appropriate ways to deal with her fears, frustrations, and problems. You must find your way through her defiance and be her partner. How? By empowering the *when, where, why, what,* and *how* of your communication with one another. As you can see in Figure 4.3, communication is one of the supporting walls of your home.

Psychiatrist William Glasser, in his book *Choice Theory*, compares what he calls the "Seven Deadly Habits" of communication with the "Seven Caring Habits." See which one reminds you more of a favorite aunt, teacher, or coach.

Seven Deadly Habits	*Seven Caring Habits*
Criticizing	Supporting
Blaming	Encouraging
Complaining	Listening
Nagging	Accepting
Threatening	Trusting
Punishing	Respecting
Bribing/rewarding to control	Negotiating differences

The "Seven Deadly Habits" can be destructive to a relationship and can harm your loving connection with others. Why? Because this form of communication is about the communicator exerting *external control*. In each case, the speaker acts as the expert and is attempting to *change* the other person's behavior. However, in reality, the only person whose behavior we can control is our own. All we can give another person is information. With the "Seven Caring Habits," we are promoting *internal control*. Our goal is to empower the other person to make the changes that will be most supportive of positive growth. This form of communication will *build connection* and be less likely to create tension, conflict, and anger. Let's take a closer look at how to shift our language from *shame, blame, and criticism* to *tolerance, empathy, and support*.

When

You have probably heard the expression "teachable moment." The truth is that the time to communicate an important lesson is *not* always when *we* think it is. Sure, what we want to say is on target, poignant, important, helpful, and bursting with brilliance. But that doesn't necessarily mean that your child is ready, willing, and able to *learn* and that you are ready to *teach*. Taking a closer look at what we have learned so far, there are several reasons why we may need to pick our moments more carefully.

- Is there *calm*? Remember, *no learning can take place* when there is stress or anxiety in the room. When the moment is heated for your child, it's as if the amygdala (the *emotional* back part of the brain) is beating strong and the prefrontal cortex (the *thinking* executive function part of the brain) is shrinking. Whether it's a moment or a true break, time spent calming down will be necessary if your child is to truly *hear* the full meaning of your message.
- Do you really know what you want to say? For the same reason as above, you may not really be able to choose your words carefully

and may instead blurt out words or speak in a manner you may regret.

- Do you have your child's full attention? Whether or not she should be hyperfocused on her latest art project when you want her to listen to the important change in afternoon plans, she is not really able in the moment to transition out of her world to join you in yours. A verbal recognition of what she is doing or a moment to let her find a pausing point may make all the difference before you begin your communication.

- Does he have "fuel in his tank"? As I discussed in Key 2, sometimes kids are emotionally dysregulated and they have already given all they have to give—especially after a full day of school. Your child may need a snack, some exercise, or some down time to refuel before being able to have a conversation about anything really important.

- Can it wait? Sometimes parents get caught up in their own needs or anxieties and don't realize that what they want to know or do, while it is important to them, is not urgent and might perhaps trigger anxiety or pressure for their child. For instance, you may be really wanting to know if your daughter found a friend to play with after school five days from now when you will need to stay late at work. Your daughter is aware of the need but is still on the fence about who to ask and has asked you to give her until midweek. Your questioning this early may satisfy your need, but undermine her need to see how things will play out at school.

- Have you set the stage? Let's say your son has been working on a math problem and has it mostly correct except for the last step. Or your daughter cleaned her room as asked but forgot to bring down the glass she was drinking from. Before you jolt them with a negative comment, if possible, take a *moment to connect*. For example, "Jacob, I see how hard you worked on this problem. It looks like the last step is incorrect. Can you take a look at what I see here?" "Emma, great effort on getting your room clean. There is just one more thing—do you see the glass over there?" *Connect before you correct.* Some people suggest the "sandwich."

Praise, then correct, and then praise again. If possible, a word of encouragement or reinforcement of the positive to end with can be helpful. "I know you will see your mistake when you look again."

Where

There are two important things to consider in terms of where you speak to your child. The first has to do with proximity. Whenever possible, try to be in the same physical space with your child when you are asking him to do something, especially if the task requires using his working memory. For instance, rather than yelling upstairs to Ian that he needs to pack up for school, you may have more success if you go to his room to at least deliver the message. This way you can see if you will need to help support a transition or help him with what and how to pack. This may seem burdensome at the moment, but it will likely allow you to teach skills and save time in the long run.

The second big "where" concern has to do with respect. As I teach teachers, there is *never, ever, ever* a good reason to embarrass or humiliate a child in front of others. If your child has done something wrong, do whatever you can to be discreet and private in delivering your message. If you do so, you are more likely to have her full attention and help foster the change you desire than you would be if the majority of your child's focus is on saving face or the boiling anger that is building toward you for the humiliation she is feeling as she senses onlookers witnessing your conversation.

Why

While it may not seem important to talk about *why* you are communicating with your child in the first place, it is still worth exploring some of the tricky issues that may be involved. First off, you may be very clear as to why you are communicating, but your child may be making his own assumptions that can derail your conversation before it gets very far. Generally, when you are not just having a conversation, there are three reasons why you may be talking to your child: to provide information, to provide feedback, or to give some sort of directive. Very often, when you have a child who is used to being redirected, reprimanded, or prodded along, he grows to *assume* that he is somehow about to be told *what to do*. So merely hearing your voice can trigger an "Oh no, what now?" reaction. To help break your child of that knee-jerk reaction, you can start with a clear statement of purpose—"I just wanted to let you know . . ." or "Can I give you some feedback?" Let him know there is nothing he needs to do or change in the moment.

If you *are* giving a directive, be clear as to whether there is a choice involved—must they do what you are asking, and if so, are you clear about when? Or is this merely a request or suggestion? "Can you start your homework now?" sounds as if there is a choice—is there? "Do you mind getting me the ketchup?" also sounds optional.

It's Not What You Say, It's *How* You Say It

The expression "A picture is worth a thousand words" is so true. Your tone, your body language, your facial expression, your hand gestures, and even your proximity to your child may have more impact than even the most carefully chosen words. Do you sound as if you are asking or accusing? Offering support or prodding? Be aware that your true feelings and intentions may be more transparent than you realize—or desire.

As you speak, keep in mind that you want to strike a balance between staying calm and appearing strong. To be strong, you must be in control of your emotions and speak with conviction—not anger, begging, or pleading. Remember, *your calm is your power!* As long as you know you have your child's attention, eye contact is not always essential—it can sometimes be too intimidating or intense for your child.

But What You Say Really Matters Too!

I will be delving more deeply into the content of powerful conversations shortly, but there are four types of communication styles that I want to highlight specifically. The first is *sarcasm*. Many people will justify their use of sarcasm as "just being funny," but in truth, while sarcasm is camouflaged as humor, it is usually a criticism, put-down, or judgment. The speaker may feel that he or she is somehow softening the blow or making light, but poking fun instead of truly communicating what might be valuable and useful feedback or information usually hurts and often embarrasses the person on the receiving end. There is no helpful conversation, and the receiver has little opportunity to safely challenge or ask for clarification or support in dealing with the issue at hand. My advice is that if what you have to say is important enough to point out, communicate in such a way that it can be safely heard and addressed.

The second communication style that tends to backfire is the *lecture*. No matter how much wisdom you may feel is in your words, chances are, sadly, that only the first few words will be heard. Be succinct and clear. Enough said!

The third style has to do with creating credibility with your child. The expression "Do as I say, not as I do" will do little to motivate good behavior, habits, or morals. Kids really model what they experience. They are watching all the time and getting their cues from you—about themselves in terms of your response to them, and about how to act based on how you handle your concerns, emotions, and so forth.

The fourth style involves making sure, whenever possible, that you use *"I" statements* rather than "you" statements and encourage your child to do the same. Speaking from the "I" is less threatening and critical. It gives you an opportunity to focus on how you are feeling rather than just the actions of your child. This is particularly important, since many kids have a hard time being sensitive or aware of another person's perspective. "When you . . . , I feel . . . , because . . . " helps them focus on how they have impacted you.

Teaching Kids the Rules of Communication

So much of the fighting that occurs at home can be reduced when we all *hear* each other—our thoughts, concerns, fears, and even just our questions. Setting basic ground rules and guidelines for *how* to have a helpful conversation will go a long way in reducing some of the daily stress. Choose a time to actively discuss with your whole family how you can *all* communicate better with one another. Whether it's during a special meal, a trip out for a fun dessert, or a Sunday night, let them know the whole conversation will take only about 15 minutes—and keep your word even if it means planning a second session. Once you discuss the basic concepts, you can post some rules and guidelines you all agree on. When you are the listener, keep in mind that, especially when you have a child with ADHD who may struggle with emotional regulation, actively listening to what your child says is so very critical in helping to defuse the situation, teach, and mediate. Here are some essential points you can cover in your family discussion:

- Are you the sender or the receiver? This seems so obvious—but by considering your role first, you can be sure to focus more carefully on both speaking your mind and hearing others' concerns. As the *sender*, you can start off by saying something to signal that you have a message to deliver. You want to make sure you have your audience's attention and their awareness that you have something to say. For instance, you might say, "I have a question" or "Is now a good time to tell you something?" Try as much as possible to speak without *shame, blame, or criticism*. Simply speak in a way that you would want someone to speak to you.

  As a *receiver*, your job is to be laser-focused on what the speaker is trying to say. Here are your three steps:

  ◊ *Mirror back what you heard.* Repeat back in your own words what you think the speaker said. This is not the time to express your own feelings about the statement, but rather to ensure that you really got the correct message. It's like the game of telephone that kids play, but this step can be very powerful in building trust and connection. Reflective listening can have a soothing effect—it gives the speaker the feeling of being truly heard and understood. "So, you are telling me that you threw the ball when Danny said you were cheating." Give the sender an opportunity to correct the receiver or add additional information if necessary. Sometimes, during this step, you may find that what your child *heard* does not match the *intent* of what you said and, in fact, reveals valuable insight into her state of mind or your relationship. For instance, if you say, "I want to you to finish your work before we go to the store," she may hear, "Mom won't let me go to the store if I don't finish," when what you really meant is that you didn't want to rush your child and wanted to wait until she had time to finish.

◊ *Validate the sender's statement.* Verbally show that you can see the sender's point of view and can accept its validity—that it is true *for the sender.* This does not imply that you agree, merely that you accept the statement. "Have I got that right? It seems that you got very upset when Danny accused you of cheating."

◊ *Empathize with the speaker.* Communicate that you connect with or really understand the emotions of the sender: "And I can imagine that you must feel . . ." or "I understand that you feel . . . . That must be really frustrating."

• *Do not interrupt the speaker.* This can be a very helpful skill to teach a child who is *impulsive.* It is important to remember that, while a child with ADHD may not be able to easily control his impulsivity, he can certainly learn coping strategies to make things easier for all involved. Perhaps writing down thoughts on a piece of paper, or putting his had up to signal his interest in speaking. Also, when you have a member of the family who has a harder time asserting or expressing himself, it is vital to allow each person to have the opportunity to be heard.

◊ *Have a hand signal.* If a person wants to ask for clarity, or is feeling confused or overwhelmed by what is being said, he can put his hand near his own face as if to say, "Please wait." Then this person can ask for clarity, a slower pace, or perhaps ask the communicator to allow one issue to be the focus at a time.

◊ *Have a "talking stick."* Whoever has the stick is the one who is the speaker.

◊ *Use a timer.* This can be especially helpful if you have a child who tends to be very talkative, has a hard time waiting his turn, or has a very hard time listening to others.

- Listen with everything you have. Don't be doing laundry, looking at a magazine, or watching TV. Your full, visible presence will make it safer for your child to speak. It has been said, "People don't care how much you know until they know how much you care."

- Resist the urge to be a problem solver. So often, when we speak, we really just want an opportunity to share how we're feeling. We're not looking for someone to tell us what to do or how to feel. In her research about teens and their relationship with their parents, researcher Ellen Galinsky found that "if [teens] feel like they're respected, if they feel like they're listened to, if they feel like they're valued, they really want adults to help shape their views about world. They want adults to tell them about the world and how it works."

◊ Gently nod or say "I see" or "Hmm."

◊ Empathize: "That sounds frustrating."

◊ Give in fantasy what you cannot give in reality: "I wish I could say there was no more homework." Then you can deal with the present reality.

◊ Ask if the sender wants your input of if he just wants to share.

- Say what you mean, and mean what you say! We all can get caught up in the moment and blurt out the first thing that comes to mind. We say things we don't mean and regret them as soon as they come out of our mouths. I once had a parent tell me that she was so angry with her child that she said, "That's it; I'm canceling your birthday party." Of course, her child knew it was an empty threat, so she only served to erode her credibility. Slow down, breathe, and then speak. If you do find you say something that you immediately regret, 'fess up. Tell the other person that you are sorry and that you got caught up in your emotions. Then calmly state what you want to say with more thought and time.

When You Have to Say No

In the next chapter, I will elaborate on what you can do if you need to say no to your child's request when there is a possibility that you might actually reconsider and say yes. But there are times when there is no question that your answer must be no. Some parents have a very difficult time dealing with their own kids' reactions when they say "no" and would rather give in than deal with the whining, crying, yelling, and so forth. Kids must learn to manage their *own* frustration with boredom, rejection, disappointment, and so forth. They will be more equipped to do so with practice and experience. Just like kids, parents sometimes need extra tools and strategies to deal with their own emotions. One strategy I find helpful is this:

Be brief
Be firm
Be gone!

In the face of your child's negative reaction when you give him a directive or say "no", you want to state your position as succinctly as possible, with a strong, clear, non-emotional voice, and then walk away from the situation. For example, you might say, in a calm but firm voice, "I said no candy until after dinner." And then walk away from your child or, if appropriate, bring your child with you and away from the situation.

We will talk in Chapter 6 about how to handle it if your child insists on following you, but for now, just practice building your determination that you *can* deal with your child's discomfort without losing your resolve or control.

A Few Final Tips

Remember, sometimes kids with ADHD seem to feed off of other people's energy. When the energy isn't there, they tend to create it. Do not move your hand up the bat—don't give energy to their excitement by adding more of your own. *You don't have to attend every fight you are invited to!* And you don't always have to take their behavior and their comments personally—sometimes it's more about the mood they're in. Be more exciting in the positive by using your praise, paying attention to the good stuff, and planning quality one-on-one time.

In the next chapter, we will challenge the premise that *"Kids do well if they want to."*

Guiding Thoughts

- Seek first to understand, then to be understood. *Listen!*
- Notice when, where, why, what, and how you speak.
- Avoid shame, blame, and criticism and replace them with *tolerance, empathy,* and *support.*
- You don't need to attend every argument you are invited to.
- Don't always take their behavior personally.

Homework

1. Remember to continue one-on-one time.
2. Plan to teach your child communication skills.
3. On the Thinkkids.org website, there is an excellent tool (the CPS Assessment and Planning Tool) that you can use to help you use to look at the "thinking skills" kids need to solve problems, be flexible, and tolerate frustration. Use this as a tool to begin identifying the situations that precipitate your child's maladaptive behaviors.

TEACH COLLABORATION

The Power of Shared Power

The beauty of empowering others is that your own power is not diminished.

— Barbara Coloroso

Before we start exploring what is behind some of the power struggles and how to reduce them, as I mentioned at the end of the last chapter, I want to challenge the conventional wisdom that *"kids do well if they want to."* Certainly, when you are dealing with kids who have ADHD, it can often be very confusing *why* they don't always do as they can, should, want, need, must, and so forth. Clearly there is a degree of *willful* behavior at play here.

Conventional wisdom told us that kids use defiant behavior to gain attention, manipulate, and coerce other people into giving in to their wishes. The belief was that kids are driven by a need for power and control and are willing to fight for it. And, that kids are not always intrinsically motivated to do what they need to, so it is up to adults to somehow create that motivation. This creed leads parents to believe that the key is to find the correct reward or punishment to motivate kids to do, as they should.

A Word About External Rewards, Punishments, and Motivation

It is often confusing what role rewards and punishments play in creating motivation. Here is what the research has shown: As long as the work or performance is within a person's expertise and control (in other words, if the child is *"response-able"*), and there is not excessive stress or pressure, rewards or threats of punishment can be effective. However, once the task calls for even rudimentary cognitive skills—in other words, if the task is more complicated and may require use of more *executive function* skill mastery— then the more we use reward or punishment, the *poorer performance becomes!* Offering a reward or threatening a punishment may actually *shut down* our child's ability to use her *executive function* skills to the best of her ability. Remember the *fight, flight,* or *freeze* response of the amygdala (the emotional brain)?

So what does motivate performance? Daniel Pink, in his book *Drive,* talks about three elements:

- Autonomy: The desire to be self-directed and have control over one's own actions
- Mastery: The desire to make progress and improve
- Purpose: The desire to find meaning and purpose; the desire to feel we are making a contribution to something greater and that we matter

This is why supporting children as they develop their interests, passions, and talents can contribute so much to their overall development. This gives them an opportunity to learn about themselves and how they learn best as well as develop their *executive function* skills as they work on mastery and feel self-value and pride.

I have found that, very often, kids with ADHD who are more behaviorally challenging have a *very strong* desire to steer their own ship at a very early age—and perhaps more so than is appropriate for some of their current self-management skills. This, as we have seen, can create tremendous stress and conflict. Think back to Henry, my client who wanted to be a rap music manager. His father was so concerned with directing his son that he didn't see how supporting his son's innate desires may have been an alternate path to helping him develop his mastery skills in a broader picture (learning about some of the skills involved in being a effective manager, for example).

It is not unusual for a child to develop a strong interest, even a passion, at an early age. Some parents worry that the time spent on this passion is "too much" or that perhaps their child is not focusing on other important things. My suggestion is to *use the passion* as a vehicle to learn other skills. For example, if your child is into a particular video game, see if there is a way to help him incorporate the character into his writing. Or he can read a book about similar characters, or how such games are developed. Use the setting and the characters to make the math problems or science concepts come to life. It may not work all the time; however, you will be showing more interest, support, and acceptance of something that is important to your child, which will go a long way in building trust and allowing you closer to his world.

Challenging Conventional Wisdom

We now understand, thanks to extensive research by Dr. Russell Barkley and others, that many children with ADHD, especially the hyperactive and impulsive type, can develop oppositional behavior as a by-product of their neurologically based disorder due to their deficits in emotional regulation.

Oppositional behaviors are not always loud or obvious, such as yelling or fighting. The challenging oppositional behaviors can show up as whining, crying, sulking, or just plain refusal. Dr. Ross Greene, associate clinical professor in the Department of Psychiatry at Harvard Medical School, and Dr. Stuart Ablon, director of Think:Kids at Massachusetts General Hospital, propose that challenging behaviors should be understood and handled the same way as other *learning disabilities*. Defiance is sometimes a learned behavior (or, as I say, a "coping technique"); it allows kids to avoid or continue as they wish, at least in the short term.

- Children want to feel *independent, competent, connected*, and *loved* . . . and they sometimes lack the skills they need to do so!
- Children are not *choosing* to be difficult any more than one chooses to have a learning disability.

In other words, we must recognize that difficult kids and adolescents are often *lacking the important skills* needed to handle *frustration*, master situations that require *flexibility* and *adaptability*, and *solve problems*.

If your child is not "doing well," meaning that she is not behaving or performing as you would expect, given her age and intelligence, Greene and Ablon (1998) propose that this indicates that the demands or expectations placed on your child exceed her capacity to respond adaptively. "Doing well" does not mean that she is always interested in complying with your requests, but rather that her response is reasonable and appropriate. The underlying premise of Greene and Ablon's work is that *"kids do well if they can."*

Is Your Child Learning to Manage His or Her Emotions?

Let's look at what happens when you have an expectation or make a request of your child. As we saw in the defiance dance (Figure 4.1), when your child *defies* your request (meaning he either *ignores, postpones without a plan, or refuses*), how you respond to your child will impact what happens next. If you give in, give up, avoid the issue, or continue to just repeat your request, your child *may* learn that when he defies, others may leave him alone to do what he wants to do or to avoid doing what he doesn't want to do. This reaction may lead to temporary emotional relief as he is released from

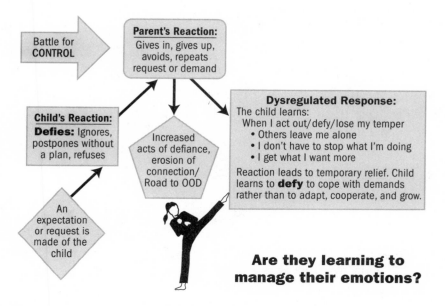

Fig. 5.1 Learning Emotional Self-Regulation

doing something undesirable. However, he is learning that defiance is a way to cope—rather than learning to adapt, deal with frustration, or develop more appropriate skills.

Whether challenging kids move on to develop diagnosable oppositional defiant disorder (ODD) depends on the way they are parented and, I believe, treated by the teachers and other significant people in their lives. I have witnessed the most caring adults who, out of love, anxiety, and misinformation, parent and teach in such a way that kids do not learn how do develop their own appropriate self-regulation skills, self-care skills, self-advocacy skills, and independent learning skills.

Reframe Your Thinking:
Kids Lack Skill, Not Will!

Through this new lens, challenging behaviors (whining, crying, refusing, yelling, sulking, etc.) are not seen as manipulative responses, but rather as *maladaptive responses*. The challenging behaviors are due to either:

- An *unsolved problem* where the child is having difficulty meeting a specific expectation (e.g., leaving the video game to do other things, sharing toys during play dates, starting or completing homework)

or

- A *lagging thinking skill*, particularly one of those needed for *flexibility, adaptability, frustration tolerance, or problem solving*.

The good news is that, with awareness and effort, major shifts in understanding and skill can happen, and kids—and yes, teens—can learn to behave and perform more successfully and productively.

In the previous chapter, I said, "How we communicate our expectations, concerns, and requests has a profound ability to trigger our children." Well, as you will see, how we communicate our expectations, concerns, and requests *also* has the ability to *teach skills, encourage respect, and inspire cooperation!* Allowing children the opportunity to explore themselves more freely can help them take ownership of and responsibility for their actions and choose to

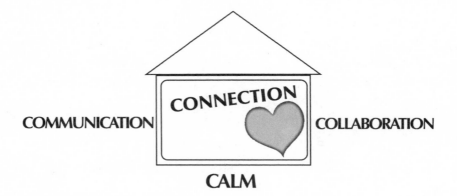

Fig. 5.2 House: Collaboration

make adjustments in who they are and what they do. The other supporting wall for our home is *collaboration* (Figure 5.2).

I incorporate the philosophy and work of the *collaborative problem solving* (CPS) model originated by Dr. Greene (and further developed and disseminated by him as well as Think:Kids at Massachusetts General Hospital under the leadership of Dr. Ablon) into the work that I do as a parent coach. In guiding you to use this model with your child, I will be asking you to include your child's thoughts, concerns, opinions, and decisions more than perhaps you have in the past. You may need to teach your child the skills she lacks step by step and provide her with support along the way. You may also need to reduce certain expectations, at least for now, as your child focuses on learning other important lessons or perhaps until she has had more opportunity to catch up developmentally to her peers.

There are a few basic beliefs in the *collaborative problem solving* model:

- Kids do well *if* they can (not just if they *want* to)!
- Your *explanation* guides your *intervention*—your belief about what is driving behavior helps you decide how to intervene
- Kids often lack the *skills* to do well, not necessarily the *will*
- These skills are often taught best using *real problems* and *conversations*—not just lectures, rewards, or punishments
- Problems are best solved when you work *proactively*—when things are calm and the problem is not pressing

If your child is struggling to behave and work appropriately, it is up to the adults in his world to help figure out what is getting in the way so they can help.

Three Plans for Approaching Unmet Expectations

When your child does not meet your expectation, you will now choose from three plans:

- Plan A: Impose your Adult will. Insist that your expectation be met before any other action is taken or there will be a consequence given.
- Plan C: Let your Child choose whether or not to comply with the expectation. Drop the expectation, at least for now.
- Plan B: Both the Adult and the Child resolve the issue. This is the *collaborative problem solving* approach.

We already know from the *defiance dance* that continually repeating the request or threatening without following through does not generally resolve issues, so these are not considered actual "plans." Before looking more closely at Plan B, I want to explore Plan A and Plan C in more detail.

There are absolutely times when it is appropriate and necessary to use Plan A. Certainly, when someone's health or safety is involved, such as when a child wants to ride a bicycle without a helmet or your child is physically hurting another person, you will likely want to have an absolute restriction on your child's actions. However, overreliance on Plan A can very often trigger challenging behavior in kids. This is because when someone *imposes their will* upon you, it requires that you have the skills to comply as well as other self-management skills (dealing with frustration, flexibility, adaptability, and problem solving.) Kids do have legitimate concerns, whether we agree with them or not. In using Plan A, we often ignore kids' concerns (or so it seems to them!). Plan A may get your expectation met in the short term; however, it may not offer you insight into *why* your child is struggling in the first place. It also will not help teach your child some of the thinking skills she is lacking.

Chances are, you have multiple problems to work out with your child. It is important to recognize that you cannot focus on every problem at once. True Plan C means you are consciously deciding that you will *not* address an issue in lieu of more important problems that need to be solved. You may be consciously deciding it's not important enough to fight over, at least in the moment; perhaps you will choose to make a suggestion rather than put out an expectation. An example here might include wearing a jacket in the colder weather. You might say, "It's very cold out; you may want to put on a jacket before going outside."

With Plan C, parents sometimes feel they are "giving in." "Giving in" is actually more like Plan A abandoned. You start off intending to impose your will, but based on your child's negative reaction, you give in or drop your expectation. If you do decide based on your child's response that you don't want to pursue your expectation, be clear and clarify the potential natural results of his or her choice. By using Plan C, you will likely reduce or avoid triggering challenging behavior, but just like with Plan A you will not gain new insight or teach thinking skills.

The Goals of Using Plan B

Rather than concentrating on gaining your child's compliance in every situation, I suggest that you shift your focus to teaching him the skills he needs to communicate his needs and wants. You don't really need to make every request that you are making right now. Chances are, he isn't complying with many of them anyway. So, for now, why not postpone the battle until you have made some changes? If you are not going to follow through and gain compliance, let go of some of your requests for the short term.

My goal in asking you to employ more of Plan B in your parenting style is to help you achieve the following:

- To reduce meltdowns and defiance
- To pursue your expectations with clear communication
- To solve problems
- To examine and reflect on the impact of your own personal parenting style (are you too lenient? too controlling?)
- To get your kids *talking* more
- To build mutual trust and connection
- To teach the lagging "thinking" skills that were introduced in the previous chapter

Assess the Reason for the Unmet Expectation

As I said earlier, challenging behaviors are due to either an unsolved problem or a lagging thinking skill. We want to try to understand what is getting in the way. I will ask you to be patient and suspend judgment while you gather information, keeping in mind that "your explanation guides your intervention" and, as you saw in Figure 4.2, we don't always *know* the full story of why kids behave as they do!

Over the next few days, develop a list of "unsolved problems" (not cleaning up after dinner, being late for the school bus, etc.). Look for the problems that are repetitive, consistent, and somewhat predictable patterns of behavior. Be as specific as you can be in describing the unmet expectation. Include information such as the following:

- When, where, with whom, and over what issues do the difficulties arise?
- What triggers your child?
- What are the settings or events?
- What are the chronic problems causing frustration for you or your child?

Also, refer back to the CPS Assessment and Planning Tool (from the Think:kids.org website) you completed in Chapter 4. Look more closely at the lagging thinking skills that contribute most to your child's challenges.

There are three main parts to Plan B, and it is important that you don't rush through each step.

Step 1: Empathy and Understanding: What Is Your Child's Concern or Perspective?

During this first step, your goal is to figure out what is getting in the way of your child's meeting your expectation, or what it is that is creating the challenging behavior. To do this, first and foremost you need to build her trust that: she is not in trouble, that you are not necessarily saying no, and that you are looking to collaborate, not to control her or the situation. You want to show that you are genuinely curious about what her concern or perspective is regarding the problem—why she is resisting following your directive or not doing what is expected of her. This requires plenty of empathy and reassurance, no matter how frustrated you may be feeling. This can have a very calming effect as the child experiences that she is truly being heard. Your child's explanation of the problem may add new information for you; perhaps it will open you up to some new insight you had not considered.

Remember, *metacognition* (self-talk), introduced in Key 1, is an *executive function* skill, and it is often lagging in children with ADHD. The more one is aware of one's thinking process, the more one can control one's mood, focus, and movement toward one's goals. Your goal is to get your child talking so that she can verbalize and recognize what she is thinking, feeling, and experiencing. You want to help her trust that by using her words to communicate her needs and concerns, she will gain more of what she wants and reduce her own anger and frustration.

During this step, you will be exploring as much as possible to gather understanding until you and your child gain clarity and insight. Once you have a clearer understanding of what your child is feeling, you can begin to respond better to the situation, but you will *not yet* try to solve the problem or offer any suggestions—that will be the third step. For now, you want to suspend judgment and just listen for *her* point of view, not yours. Explore the who, what, where, and when of the unsolved problem.

- Try to externalize the problem and talk about what you observe. Stick with the facts, not your assumptions.
- When possible, avoid "why" questions that may put your child on the defensive. Instead, use "how" questions to touch upon your child's thoughts, feelings, and intentions—for example, "I notice you didn't clean your room" instead of "I notice you avoid cleaning your room."
- Sometimes it can be helpful to explore in fantasy what you can-

not explore in reality as a way of getting your child to talk about reality. For example, you could say, "Wouldn't it be great if I could wave a magic wand and make homework disappear?"

- Be sure you are not disguising your opinion and not offering premature solutions in your questions—for example, by saying, "Don't you think that by waiting until later . . . ?" or "Next time, wouldn't it be a good idea to . . . ?"

- Avoid sarcasm, shame, blame, and criticism—for example, "If only you would . . ." or "Gee, that plan worked out well, didn't it?"

- As much as it may pain you to see your child struggle, you don't want to downplay her concern as not real or important—for example, by saying, "Oh, it's no big deal, really."

- Be willing to acknowledge and take responsibility for your role in the problem. For example, you could say, "I notice I'm . . . I see that it's not helping. I'd like to come up with another way and would like your help."

- Slow down and allow for silence. You want to get your child talking! Keep in mind that you do not have to agree with your child's concern or perspective, just understand it.

Listen

Do not have an opinion while you listen because frankly, your opinion doesn't hold much water outside of Your Universe.

Just listen.

Listen until their brain has been twisted like a dripping towel and what they have to say is all over the floor.

—Hugh Elliot

You will need to call upon the listening skills we talked about in the previous chapter. Also, here are some specific types of questions and statements that might help move the conversation along:

- *Reassurance, empathy and validation.* Especially if your child gets agitated or shuts down, reassurance that that he is not in trouble or being controlled is vital. A soft, heartfelt comment that shows you are empathic to his struggle can be helpful. The key here is to remember that empathy and validation are not the same as agreement. It does not mean that you concur with his position or viewpoint. It is simply showing that you understand and accept his perspective. Make sure you are being genuine and not just holding back on the punishment. Be willing to be wrong about your belief about what your child is thinking, feeling, and so forth, and let him correct you.

◊ "You make sense."
◊ "I'm not saying no . . . I'm not saying you have to."
◊ "I'm not saying you can't."
◊ "I really want your opinion, not just what you think I want to hear."
◊ "I know you are trying hard."
◊ "You are not in trouble here; I just want to mention that I notice that something about doing homework isn't working for you."
◊ "I just want to understand—I'm sure you must have a good reason."
◊ "What's the worst thing that can happen if you tell me what you're thinking?"

• *Clarifying questions.* Clarify what you are hearing to ensure that you truly understand and to help them elaborate further. "How so?" and "Can you say more about that?" can elicit more information and clarity. When possible, provide a name for the feeling the child is experiencing so that she can begin to expand her vocabulary for the emotions she is feeling.

◊ "Can you give me an example?"
◊ "How come?"
◊ "I don't quite understand. I'm confused. Can you help me understand?"
◊ "Why does this cause a problem at home but not at school?"
◊ "What part of doing homework is hard?"

- *Educated guessing questions.* If you feel that your questions aren't getting you anywhere, then ask if it is okay if you guess. Keep in mind that you can only offer your guess and must be open to your child's disagreeing. You will need to check with your child to see if you are accurately grasping how she feels. Often, when you guess, it opens the door for the child to express more accurately how she is thinking, feeling, and so forth.

  ◊ "Mind if I take a guess?"
  ◊ "I imagine you are feeling . . . [hurt, angry, sad, etc.]."
  ◊ "Let me know if you think I'm getting warm."
  ◊ "Some other kids I know . . ."
  ◊ Play Twenty Questions.

- *Acknowledgment of feelings/reflective listening:* Help your child name her feelings and mirror what she says.

  ◊ "Are you saying . . . ?"
  ◊ "Am I right that . . . ?"

Once you feel you really fully understand your child's concern and/or perspective, then you are ready to move on to the next step of CPS.

Step 2: Define the Problem: What Is Your Adult Concern or Perspective?

Now that you have clarified your child's concerns and perspective, it's time to express your concern. But wait—what *is* your concern? Articulating your concern is not always as easy as it would seem. Why are you concerned about the issue? Why is it important to you? Do you and your partner agree about the concern and if not, are you ready to collaborate with each other? (You may want to have a CPS conversation with your partner to make sure!) I recommend that you practice expressing your concern out loud to yourself or perhaps your partner or another adult. It is not always as easy to articulate concerns as it may seem.

Be sure to revisit your beliefs regarding your role in your child's success, happiness, and so forth to help you best verbalize your position. You want to clarify your *concern* verses your *expectation*—for example, "The thing is, my *concern* is that when you don't clean your room, it seems to impact your ability to find the things you need" versus "I *expect* you to keep your room clean and I notice that you are not." Both may be valid positions—it is your prerogative as a parent to decide your rules/expectations. However, each statement will lead to a different discussion and potential solution.

It is important to make sure that you are not putting forth your *solution* at this point, but rather that you are expressing your concern. Your child does not have to *care* about your concern; she just needs to take it into consideration.

Step 3: The Invitation to
Brainstorm a Solution

Now that you and your child have a clearer understanding of each other's concerns, the work of generating a solution can begin. I like to use the image of you and your child now sitting on the *same side* of the couch looking at the problem across the room. The air is now, hopefully, a little less emotionally charged as you work *together* toward a solution that addresses *both of your concerns*. Depending on your relationship leading up to this point, you may have some proving to do that you *will address your child's concern* and not just control this decision.

You can start by asking your child to restate both of the concerns, or you can begin yourself if he struggles or does not want to: "I wonder if there is a way that . . . " or "How can we . . . ?" Now you can both brainstorm to come up with a solution that meets both your concerns. If possible, ask your child to offer the first suggestion. Here are some guidelines for effective brainstorming:

- Consider and write down all ideas and agreements with specific "how's" and descriptive terms, regardless of whether they are "Silly" or "Sensible."
- No judgment or evaluation of any ideas is offered—that will come later.
- Be optimistic and patient.

You are looking for a win–win solution—one that is *doable* and *durable* over time and one that addresses each person's concern. If the discussion becomes too stressful, consider taking a break and returning when you have each had some time to think and calm down.

Parents sometimes tell me that they tried CPS and were unsuccessful. To make this work, you will need to make sure that the agreement you come up with is not only possible, but that you are making sure to give it the support it needs to work. And you must add in accountability and opportunity for adjustment. This is a vital step in the whole process.

When you come to an agreement, set up in advance:

- What will we see if this is working?
- What will we do if this is working?
- What will we see if this is not working?
- What will we do if this is not working?

Write down the agreement and a date to meet again to assess how the plan is working. You want an opportunity to acknowledge and celebrate success, as well as to make adjustments if things are not working well. Agree to come back to the table to voice concerns, rather than resorting to arguing, shame, blame, or criticism if the solution isn't working.

Sometimes, your child will come up with a solution that in your gut you feel may not work, but he is *so* convinced will. Remember, there is a lot of growing and maturing your child still needs to go through that will only happen with experience. Especially in the tween and teen years, there may be a certain amount of what I refer to as "bravado" and "magical thinking." For example, when faced with the problem that she isn't getting to school on time, your daughter may say, "I am just going to try harder and I know I will succeed." You may want to give that "solution" a trial run—so you will be able to come back to the table to further assess *why* that solution may not have worked.

Getting Started With the Process of Collaborative Problem Solving

Now that you see the process of CPS, take a look at the list of unsolved problems and lagging skills that you developed. Identify the problem behavior you want to work on. Remember to separate out the *problem* from the *behavior* so you can focus on the problem, rather than a behavior as a *result* of a problem. The *behavior* is the child's action—yelling, fighting, complaining, forgetting. The *problem* is what they do it about—homework, chores, cleaning, helping. This is more descriptive than saying your child is lazy, unmotivated, or disrespectful. Parents are often tempted to start using Plan B on the biggest problems. This can be too ambitious at first and is likely to be unsuccessful. Instead, choose a problem that is small and can be clearly defined. You may want to ask your child what she wants to work on.

If you have a strong, connected relationship with your child where you can engage in helpful conversations, you may want to start with the problems that cause the most frequent or challenging behavior, one whose solution will help reduce stress all around and help things run more smoothly. However, if your relationship is stressed or strained and communication is difficult, you may want to start with a problem that may be easier to successfully resolve or that your child is most invested in resolving. Choose one where you feel you might have an easier time teaching your child the process and might have some "easy" success (e.g., remembering to hang up a coat).

At an appropriate age and developmental level, teach her the basic process of collaborative problem solving:

- You each state your own concern
- You work hard to understand and not judge the other person's concern, using your best listening skills
- You work together to brainstorm a solution
- You agree to revisit the solution at a preplanned time to make sure it is working

If helpful and appropriate, you can acknowledge your participation in the problem as a way to entice your child and bring her in. ("I realize I have been nagging you about . . . "). Let your child know that you don't want to fight each time there is a disagreement between you. You might also verbalize that you recognize that your child is maturing and you would like to give her an opportunity to participate in more of the decisions that involve her. Remember to review the rules of having a good conversation from the previous chapter if necessary.

You may want to practice CPS using a hypothetical situation. For example, Mom wants to buy a boat and Dad says, "No way." Imagine how Mom feels being told "no" when she feels she should have a say, too. How can this conflict become a conversation where some kind of solution can be found that satisfies both Mom and Dad? After some careful conversation that focuses on each of their *concerns*, it turns out we learn the following:

MOM'S CONCERNS
- She really enjoys being on the water
- She likes to be in a place where there is nature and open space

DAD'S CONCERNS
- Boats can be expensive to purchase and maintain
- He doesn't want to feel tied into boating so often if they make such an investment

- He doesn't want to feel pressured to entertain his family and friends
- He has never really felt comfortable on the water

After considering some ideas, Mom and Dad decide that they will rent a kayak from time to time. Dad agrees to try it out. Sometimes, Mom can go with friends or family, sometimes with just Dad, and sometimes alone.

Through this process, I have had many parents recognize, to their credit, that it is the they who are having a hard time letting go and relinquishing some of their control and that, after a few rocky starts perhaps, their child has risen to the occasion and felt stronger and more confident as a result.

If your child is reluctant to participate or if the Plan B conversation is just not going well, consider the following:

- What is getting in the way of your child's talking to you?
- Is this a good time to talk? You may not get far now by pushing and will build more trust and goodwill by waiting.
- Are your "fuel tanks" empty?
- Does he need time to explore his concern more?
- Are you using a "disguised" Plan A?
- Does he trust your sincerity and intention?
- Are you using shame, blame, or criticism?
- Are you using sufficient reassurance and empathy?
- Have you acknowledged your role in the problem?
- Would a small incentive to try the process help?

If your child is still reluctant to come to the table with honest intention, let him know that it is still your preference to collaborate; however, if he is not willing, then you are left with no choice but to impose your will (Plan A). "I am willing to discuss this problem and come to an agreement. However, if you won't work with me in good faith, then I will make the decision that I believe is best. It's your choice." Also, if your child keeps saying he will talk but doesn't follow through with a time, you may have to take that same position of stating that you will need to impose your will at a certain time.

Emergency Plan B: When You Must Resolve the Conflict in the Moment

Plan B is most definitely best when it can be done proactively, when the problem is not pressing. There are times, of course, when the issue is urgent and must be dealt with immediately. This will certainly go more smoothly once your child is familiar with the CPS process. Once your child has developed trust that you genuinely *will* hear her concern, you can teach her my "one-shot" deal:

"You've got one shot to plead your case. Calmly tell me your concern without arguing or yelling so that I understand why it's important to you and why you think I should change my mind. I give you my word that I will listen and give serious consideration to your concern. Then I will make a decision. Once the decision is made, the decision stands. There will be no more discussion and we move on."

Stay calm and don't "put your hand up the bat" and get into a power struggle. If you find that this same issue or a similar one keeps coming up, then it might be time for a proactive Plan B.

What Is There to Gain?

Plan B offers a different approach to handling unmet expectations. It is not simply negotiating a compromise. As you will see, it is much more powerful than that. Our objective must be to teach our kids the skills they lack, not just to become more effective in imposing our will and ensuring that our kids have enough incentive to comply. If you look over the CPS Assessment and Planning Tool, you will see that *just by having the collaborative conversation,* you are helping your child develop skills that she may be struggling with.

Parents sometimes wonder when they should begin teaching *collaborative problem solving*. My feeling is that you should begin as early as you can. By starting with your child at a young age, you are teaching her the language of "appropriate disagreement" so that later on she is not defiant. She has the proper tools to use to disagree, negotiate fairly, and advocate for herself. By including your child in the conversation, you are helping her build her communication skills, her problem solving skills, her ability to be more flexible, and her ability to handle frustrating situations.

Parents also question whether using CPS takes too long or gives over too much power to their child. Experience has shown that the time invested in slowing down and including them in the process pays off as children learn to trust their parents and themselves as capable problem solvers. It can also *greatly reduce the time that is spent arguing.* Listening to your child's concerns and objections does not mean you have given up any of your parental authority; you are simply acknowledging your child's viewpoint and value. Your involvement with her could help prevent a meltdown, gain more cooperation, and help her build her confidence and trust in others. She will also learn the importance of *integrity* and keeping her word.

Remember, your goal is not to agree with each other's concerns or perspectives—just to understand them. Keep in mind that *your explanation guides your intervention*—so how you both talk about the problem will be a vital contributor to how you both deal with the problem. The process of CPS takes time and patience. It may feel forced and awkward at first, but it is the best way I know of to teach skills and solve problems!

Guiding Thoughts

- *"Kids do well if they can."* If he could, he would.
- You don't need to attend every argument you are invited to.

- Choose your plan before you speak.
- Ask questions—don't just offer solutions!
- Shoot for conversations, not confrontations.
- Invite your child to be part of the solution instead of the focus of the problem.
- Without calm, he cannot learn.
- Use Plan B proactively.
- Shoot for improvement, not perfection.
- Acknowledge his effort, willingness, and progress to try as he learns how to handle disagreements more appropriately.
- Keep faith in the process; if you slip back, try again.
- Change takes energy, practice, patience, experience, and time for all concerned. It's hard!
- Avoid shame, blame, and criticism.

Seek first to Understand, then to be Understood.
—Stephen Covey, *The Seven Habits of Highly Effective People*

Homework

1. Continue to have your one-on-one time. You may find that at the end of spending some quality time with your child, you are able to have some good Plan B conversations.
2. Generate a list of Plan B conversations you want to have and choose just one to start with.
3. Incorporate your active listening skills into your regular conversations with your family.

BE CLEAR AND CONSISTENT

Predictability *Really* Helps

Decide what you want, decide what you are willing to exchange for it, establish your priorities and go to work.
— H. L. Hunt, oil tycoon

Did you ever notice that within one family, siblings can be so completely different? They may have very different interests, talents, passions, *and behaviors*—even when being parented by the same parents! Kids are each born with a unique temperament and a unique neurological makeup, which greatly impacts how they are equipped to respond to their world. As I mentioned previously, I have found that kids very often fall into two camps: those who are generally compliant and able to solve differences relatively easily, and those who are more strong-willed and challenging to parent.

Parents who are very strict and authoritative are often very effective at being consistent. Their rules are very clear, as are their consequences for violation of those rules. This style of parenting may work fine for innately compliant kids who are often motivated by pleasing their parents *and* have the skills to do so. In reality, for kids who are innately compliant, most parenting styles will be effective.

Some people think that, when working with kids with ADHD, clarity and consistency is the most important place to start. After all, having a structured, predictable environment means kids know what is expected of them, and then they can just do as they are told or suffer the consequences. Right? Well, as you probably already know from your own experience, easier said than done!

Even though there are tremendous benefits for some kids, a strict and authoritative parenting style can often create endless power struggles, anger, and rebellion from strong-willed ADHD kids.

Often, even at a very young age, kids with ADHD feel a tremendous need to have a great deal of control over their lives. They often respond to strict parenting by becoming more oppositional and obstinate. However, these same kids, with their lags in *executive function* skills, are not always able to plan and follow through with their great intentions, nor do they always respond to the same situation in the same way each time for sometimes unknown or nonobvious reasons. As we have seen, how we talk with our kids and our willingness to let them share in some of the decision making can greatly impact their behavior and compliance. For these kids, parenting style has a huge and vital impact on their growing nature.

Recognizing the importance of flexibility and adaptability in our own parenting style does not take parents off the hook from being concerned with clarity and consistency; in fact, it is by *being* clear and consistent that we are able to help kids build the skills they are lacking and develop the emotional self-regulation they require to be successful in life. Therefore, we can add part of the roof to our home (Figure 6.1).

For kids to be held accountable for their actions and responsibilities, they need to be aware of and understand what is expected of them. Very often, parents do not give thought to what they want their kids to do, or not do, until there is a specific problem. As a parent, you cannot be clear and consistent without knowing what your bottom line is—your nonnegotiable rules. There is a cartoon I once saw that depicts two people looking over a contract. One person hands the other a pen and says, "Sign here to indicate you have no idea what you are signing." This, in essence, is what we

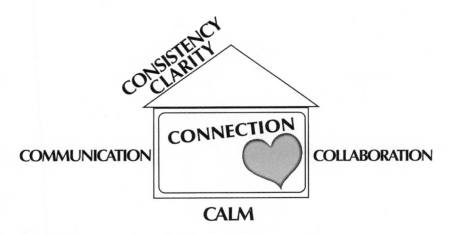

Fig. 6.1 House: Clarity and Consistency

are saying to our kids when we are *not clear up front* with our rules and expectations. For example, do your kids know the rules and expectations regarding the following?

- Bedtime (being ready, being in bed, all screens off and lights out)
- Cleaning up (when, what is required)
- Homework (when done, where, parental involvement [how much help, supervision])
- Use of electronics (phones, computers, TVs, tablets, etc.)
- Privacy (when doors must remain open, or can be closed)
- Dinner time (length of time required to stay seated)
- Language (what is acceptable)
- Chores
- How to handle disagreements
- Play dates (how often, when, who arranges)

These kids *really* need to know what to expect. What are the basic rules of their universe? I have found that very often, rules and expectations are only discussed only once there is a problem—and at this point the negative habits and adjustments necessary are much harder to address.

Why Clarity and Consistency *Really* Matter

Many kids like video games. Why? In addition to being visually stimulating, they are, in certain ways, predictable and consistent. And they provide immediate feedback. If you lose a particular challenge, you lose—all the yelling, screaming, negotiating, or crying won't earn you a new chance or "life." As a result, kids spend their energy *learning the rules of the game* rather than fighting them because the rules *won't and don't change!*

There was a study I learned about years ago where babies were observed playing on a beach at a safe distance from the water with their parents close by. The researchers studied the difference in how long the babies played comfortably when one variable was changed. In one set, there were no particular markers between the babies and the moms. In the second set, there were simply four poles set around the babies in four corners, with the moms standing just outside the imaginary boundaries, the same distance as in the first scenario. The other group had no poles or markers. It was concluded that the babies within the imaginary boundaries played significantly longer and seemed more relaxed. Somehow, innately, they felt safer knowing there were boundaries. The same can be said of most people: They work better within the confines of known and reasonable boundaries—clear, predictable expectations that they are able to follow.

In addition to the benefits of clarity and consistency for most kids, there are specific reasons why kids with ADHD may require this structure even more.

- *Time management.* With their challenges in internally anticipating and measuring time, the more kids know about *when* they are expected to do something, complete something, or be somewhere, the better.
- *Working memory.* By having clear guidelines that are visible, consistent, and predictable, kids do not have to rely as much on holding rules and expectations in their heads.

- *Emotional regulation.* There is less room for disagreement and argument when the rules and expectations are clearly defined!
- *Transitions.* One thing we know about most kids with ADHD is that they have a difficult time with *transitions*: stopping one activity and switching to a different activity at a defined time. Often this is due to *"hyperfocus"*—their deep and intense concentration on a particular task or item. It can also be due to ambivalence or reluctance to begin doing the next required activity. Or, their difficulty starting a new task. See the box below for some tips, tools, and strategies to ease transition time.

Remember, kids do well *if* they can. Our goal is to help them learn to manage their emotions and develop their executive function skills. It will be helpful to maximize the *external supports* you offer to help them develop the *internal regulation* necessary so that they can *respond* rather than *react* to life's demands.

Facilitating Smooth Transitions

Preparation, guidance, and connection are the keys to easing transitions. Following are a few tips:

- *Daily overviews.* Let your child know in advance what her schedule is so she is not surprised. This is important for a few reasons. First, it allows her to plan her time more efficiently. She knows when she can potentially make social plans or needs to make changes in anticipation of an upcoming test or project. Second, if there is something expected of her at a particular time, there is time for her to voice a concern or make the necessary adjustments. That is, she can discuss possibilities with you in advance, which is better than having to adjust in the moment when there is time pressure and changes are harder to make. It is also helpful to let your child know in advance if *you* will not be available to her for rides or homework help so that she can anticipate this and plan in advance. I recommend that kids use their agenda book as their overall calendar so as to keep any appointments or plans they have all in the same place. You can help them learn how to be discreet about certain appointments (doctor's, etc.) that they may not want others to see on their calendar.

- *Timers and clocks.* Any time your child needs to be responsible for time, she must have a tool to use. Simply giving a verbal warning of "Be down in 5 minutes" is *not sufficient* for a child who has no internal sense of time. Be sure to have easy-to-read clocks in all major areas of the house where your child hangs out: bedroom, bathroom, playroom, near the TV or computer, and kitchen. Although kids should know how to read an analog clock, I recommend using digital clocks. I have found that most kids with ADHD respond better to seeing an actual number, since time does not "speak to them" in an analog clock. Also, have a few easy-to-use kitchen timers on hand and let your child have one as well. This way, when you say "5 minutes," either you or your child can set the time. For kids who are able to read a clock, you may start by saying "What time is it?" and then say, "Okay, at 5:15 (or "in 10 minutes") come down for dinner." This way, everyone is clear about the expectation and you are helping your child be responsible—less nagging from the adult!

- *Ample warning.* Even with the proper tools, kids still need to have a warning in enough time when they are expected to change activities. Five minutes may not be sufficient for them to finish the game they are in or the show they are watching. If you notice you are having the same battle each time and it's a pattern, use your *collaborative problem solving* skills with your child to durably solve the problem.

- *Acknowledgment of what they are doing.* Before you ask your child to do something different, notice what she is currently doing. It is courteous and will make her feel valued, and it can teach her to do the same before they interrupt you, too. "Jessie, I see you are involved in reading your book. I need you to help me unload the groceries."

- *Choosing a stopping point.* Stopping an activity is not always easy, especially when hyperfocus is involved. When you let your child know that it will shortly be time for her to leave her activity, suggest that she figure out a good point to stop her current activity—two more turns each in the game, four more pages in the book, ten more beads on the necklace, and so forth.

- *Joining in.* I once saw a woman standing patiently in the back of a room after a presentation I had given was over and most of the people had gone. I noticed she was standing near a boy around 10 years old, seemingly waiting for him. I approached her and asked if she needed anything, figuring that if she was at one of my lectures about parenting kids with ADHD, there was a good chance she needed some support. She said, "No, I'm just waiting for my son to finish his video game." I smiled inside, knowing this sweet woman was probably trying to be patient and not make a scene—but also knowing there was little chance her son would ever "finish" his video game. As I recommended above, I suggested that she go sit by him and observe where he was and take interest in that moment of the game. Then she could ask him where a good stopping point was and show interest as he got there. Within 2 minutes they got up together to leave, and she smiled at me on the way out. It may not always go this smoothly, but sometimes kids need a little extra support to be successful. So whether it's joining them to see the fish in the fish tank and planning when you can revisit, or admiring the building they are working on as you help them prepare to transition, a few moments of connection can go a long way.

- *A routine that signals it's time to start.* Just like professional baseball players have their routine when they approach the plate to bat and chefs have their routine to set their kitchen, help your child develop a routine to prepare to work: clearing off her desk, gathering her favorite snack, petting the dog one last time, and so forth. Again, if she has a hard time starting consistently, perhaps discuss with her what might make things easier for her.

What Are Your Parenting Values?

Each parent experienced being parented differently. The way we were parented informs and guides our own parenting style. In some ways, we may mimic our parents (intentionally or not); in some ways we may aim to do the opposite of what our parents did! When both parents don't work from the same set of rules and values, this can lead to a situation where kids either play one parent off the other or behave differently in the presence of one or the other parent.

If you have a partner with whom you are parenting your child, it is vital that you both explicitly discuss your beliefs about core issues and different styles and do what it takes to reach agreement on how to parent *as a team*. Explicitly discuss your nonnegotiable rules and expectations. If you don't, your differences are likely to come to light when there is stress and strain, and we know that *no learning or problem solving* can happen under those conditions!

The divorce rate among parents of kids with special needs is significantly higher than in the rest of the population. Chances are, this is not only due to the stress of the challenging child, but also because parents are forced to face issues and differences in one another more than when parenting goes along more smoothly. While other couples are socializing with one another, you might find yourselves canceling or avoiding social plans as you tend to your kids, or spending your "date" time discussing your kids and how to face the next challenge. With the added stress, you must take the time and care to address and resolve differences and tend to your relationship. And keep in mind that the differences between you and your partner can add stress and confusion for your child as well.

When I work with couples, I always remind them that they *each* love their child tremendously; however they may have different beliefs and perspectives on how to handle different issues. It's important to put egos aside and work toward resolution of the issues *without* involving your child. Be discreet and supportive of one another—this isn't an easy journey for anyone. Use your *col-*

laborative problem solving skills to work out your differences. And, if necessary, seek the support of an outside person to help you hear one another more clearly and mediate your differences.

Rights Versus Privileges

One of our responsibilities as parents is to teach our kids what life is about in the real world. We need to parent in a way that does not "bend the universe" by having drastically different things happen in response to how we act at home versus out in society. Somehow, we need to create an environment at home that gradually models and prepares them for what will be expected of them as adults and what they can expect back from the universe.

For the most part, I strongly believe that we need to help kids develop their own pathways and give them plenty of autonomy in doing so. However, along that road we still need to ensure that they are developing good habits, morals, and opportunities while they may be too young to appreciate the impact of their intentions and behaviors.

We explored the complex issue of *motivation* in Key 5. Motivation is easiest when someone feels a *sense of autonomy, desires mastery*, and *has a sense of purpose* regarding what he is doing. Unfortunately, motivation is not always present in our kids when we want or need it to be. As I have mentioned before, some kids are generally innately compliant and will do as they are asked to please you and other adults. But some kids need to have more motivation than that! Certainly, a 7-year-old may feel no tremendous desire to develop mastery or have a great sense of purpose in cleaning up his room. We may have discussions with him, using our best communication skills and Plan B conversations to understand his concerns and ensure that he understands our concerns. But *if we want to pursue our expectation*, we may need to provide more incentive to motivate him. After all, for many people, the reason they go to work is not the fame, pride, or fun—it's the money!

One important distinction we must help kids understand is the difference between a *right* and a *privilege*: what is reasonable for kids to expect, and what the privileges are that we provide for them. If we are not clear with this distinction, we confuse them about what they are entitled to, both at home and in life. And this will become a more vital concern as your child grows if you decide to withhold material items or opportunities based on his behavior.

I believe that all kids have the right to security, food, shelter, the opportunity for a proper education, *and love*. While it may seem logical, then, to assume that everything else is a privilege and therefore fair game for restricting, it's more complex than that. You will want to consider the implications and unintended consequences before you enact any restrictions. For example, it may be a privilege to take guitar lessons; however, this may be the one area of life where your daughter feels especially competent and passionate. Also, will there be a financial burden to bear if a lesson is canceled, and if so, who will suffer that loss? How about participating in practice for the soccer team? Are others relying on her? Will she suffer long-term consequences for missing the one practice? How about that play date? Was this an important opportunity for your socially shy or awkward son? Is another parent relying on you for her own son or to free her up for an appointment? These are all areas of concern that I encourage you to proactively discuss with your partner and your child. Remember, kids' minds are "under construction." Whenever possible, do not remove privileges that are developmentally beneficial—until you have tried everything else, as we will discuss in the next chapter.

Most parents have certain policies about what their kids can do, use, and have and other areas where they have no policy and may not give much thought, direction, or guidance. Often, especially when kids are younger and the perceived negative effect is minimal, parents are lenient with certain activities and opportunities, such as time spent watching TV, use of electronics, play dates, trips for ice cream, purchasing of toys, and so forth. As a result, much is given to our kids without regard or connection to their behavior. It is often only once a problem develops that parents consider what leverage they may have to correct a negative situation.

In the next chapter, I will help you determine when, how, and with what you can use leverage for impacting your child's behavior. However, for now I must encourage you to determine for yourself what you view as your child's rights, and what you view as his privileges. This will help you determine what you are willing to restrict if need be.

A Note About Gifts

When children are given gifts, especially some of the more expensive, elaborate gifts like phones or gaming systems, kids may feel that they are theirs to use whenever and however they want. If you child receives a gift that you anticipate might cause problems regarding when and how it is used, you may want to state from the start that while the item is hers, use of the item may be discretionally based on certain conditions that you set forth. It is better to have the discussion and agreement at the beginning then if a problem arises.

Developing a List of Incentives

It is very helpful to *proactively* develop a list of potential incentives to have on hand to help motivate your child toward positive behavior. You should get your child's input in creating this list so that he can feel invested in earning the rewards. It will also give you insight into things that may motivate him that you had not considered. The following questions may give you some helpful "talking points":

- What are your child's favorite restaurants or dessert places?
- What special games or activities does your child enjoy?

- What special toy, book, or other material item might be exciting to earn? (Try not to make this an item that would take significant time to work toward.)
- What would your child like to get *out* of doing? (cleaning room, other chores)
- What special privilege would motivate your child?

Have fun and be creative in developing this list—pillow fights, mini golf, late night. Keep in mind that one of the greatest incentives (that is often overlooked and sometimes not admitted or acknowledged in older children) is time spent with you, their loving parent. When possible, as you develop this list, see if *you* can be included in the payoff—shopping for the reward together, watching a movie together, and so forth.

To Be Responsible, They Must Be Response-*Able*!

Just because your child *should* be able to keep track of her time, materials, and obligations doesn't mean that she is ready yet. Remember that ADHD is a *developmental disorder*. Sometimes it is helpful to have your own *504 plan* for the home. You want to help your child compensate and learn "how" rather than insisting on competent performance. Our goal is not just compliance; it is helping our kids develop proper life skills. This means you must be willing to make accommodations and modifications to help your child be successful with her responsibilities.

There are two ways you can help compensate for weak and developing executive function skills:

1. *Modify the expectation:* Rather than having your child do *all* of a particular task, you can break it down and have him be increasingly responsible for each part. For example, instead of having him make the whole bed before school, require that he pull the blanket up and put the pillow where it belongs. This way, he is

still getting used to setting aside time, following directions, and creating order.

2. *Modify the environment.* When children are very young, we modify the home environment with safety locks on cabinets, cushioning harsh corners, etc. For kids with ADHD, sometimes an environment may create too many distractions or challenges for your child. While some parents think about removing all distractions from a bedroom, this can be frustrating for a child who enjoys feeling his "stuff" in his space and enjoying the sense of independence that comes with having one's own domain. Instead, I recommend discussing with your child how he can modify his environment, as necessary, to accomplish what he needs to do. For example, having a trifold poster board (like the ones kids use to display projects) can be used at the desk, or at any other work space, to block out distractions.

Just What Are Your Child's Responsibilities?

As I started out this chapter, I showed that if you are clear and up front about what you expect from your child, it will be a lot easier to know when there are areas in need of improvement. Once you have developed your list of routine responsibilities, you will want to make sure you communicate them clearly. You want to signal to your child that you are not looking to impose a whole new set of expectations. Simply, you want to clarify and articulate what her responsibilities are so that there is no misunderstanding. Rather than listing every expectation, I suggest starting with the most basic—perhaps what she is already doing—and including one or two that you want to see improvement on. If any of the items are new, then be sure to discuss them in more detail and see if your child anticipates any difficulty in following through with the task. Depending on her age and development, you may want to break each responsibility up into steps. For example, for a young child, the list might include a morning and evening checklist:

MORNING CHECKLIST
- Eat breakfast
- Brush and floss my teeth
- Wash my face
- Brush my hair
- Get dressed
- Make my bed

You can ask your child to decorate the list. If she is too young to read, either use pictures or take a picture of your child doing the activity and include it on the chart. You can simply laminate the chart and have her check it off as she completes the item each morning.

For an older child or teen, the list might include less detail, but more responsibilities:

DAILY RESPONSIBILITIES
- Hang up coat in the closet when you get home
- Clear the dishes after we all finish eating
- Put your dirty clothes in the hamper before you leave for school
- Set alarm for the morning
- Straighten up the bathroom

Each of the items listed should be *specific, achievable, and not behavior based* (not related to language used, fighting, etc.). Also, if time is involved, be sure to indicate that in the expectation and provide a tool for measuring the time. For example, one item might be "Get dressed by 8:15 a.m.," with clocks and timers being provided where needed.

Keep in mind that it may take months to develop a new habit, and continued support and cueing may be necessary to help the process along. If it is in an area in which your child struggles to comply, ask him what might make it easier for him. Perhaps he can set an alarm, or you can agree to offer one reminder. Remember your communication and CPS skills! Perhaps this might be a time when you need to offer a small incentive to help your child develop the new habit of compliance. Help your child be successful! For the moment, don't be concerned what to do if your child *doesn't* comply—we will tackle that issue shortly.

A Thought About Chores

One of the best ways to create order and balance at home is to have kids contribute to the family by doing chores. I am going to define *chores* as tasks or responsibilities your child has that impact not just her, but your whole family. For instance, cleaning her room may impact her; however, it will not make any difference to her sister if she does it or she doesn't. A *family chore* would be something like taking out the garbage, setting the table for dinner, or emptying the dishwasher. Very often, especially when there is a lot of non-compliance and stress in a household, parents forgo asking their kids to do any family chores. Some parents even avoid asking for basic help, such as getting the tomato sauce from the pantry or helping unpack the car after a trip to the grocery store.

It is up to parents to determine what chores should be shared by family members. These decisions will vary based on values, economics, need, and time available. I do recommend that at a minimum, you establish one age-appropriate chore that impacts the family. In addition to the obvious importance of your child's contribution, the act of giving her these responsibilities sends the message that she must contribute to the family and gives you ample opportunity to help her work on her planning, managing, and cooperating skills.

In the family chores, you may want to include a once or twice a year scheduled "clean out." This is where each person goes through his or her personal belongings to see what there might be to give away or throw away. As a family chore, it can include going through the playroom and the garage. It's a great opportunity to help kids recognize their growth, physically and emotionally, as they evaluate what things they may have outgrown. It's also a good time to create or reestablish order and cleanliness. This can be done at birthday time, at the change of seasons, or around major holidays.

And About Their Room . . .

Many parents end up in major battles over the cleanliness and orderliness of their child's room. Especially once kids reach the tween and teen years, I recommend having an explicit agreement regarding what is required versus what is suggested. Especially for kids with ADHD who struggle with organization and time management, not only can a room get out of hand, but also it can become a major project to bring back to order. *If* you find that the state of your child's room is negatively impacting his ability to function (find things, do homework, socialize), then you may want to have explicit expectations in place. Some parents find that having a once-a-week rule is helpful (e.g., the room must be clean Sunday nights by 7 p.m.). Of course, be clear that you both agree what "clean" means. You may also want to have definite rules regarding food and beverages in the room if you find they are not being removed in a timely fashion. Regarding laundry, you may want to have the rule that if your child wants his clothes washed, he is responsible to get them to the hamper by a time you determine in advance. The life lesson he will learn by not having his favorite shirt clean when he wants it is an easy one for you to not get involved in.

As for doing laundry, kids are capable of learning how to do laundry at a very young age, especially with your help. If they are not responsible for doing laundry on a regular basis, you may consider having them be responsible during vacation and the summer when they are not "working." It's great prep for when they go away from home for college or otherwise and can give you a well-deserved break.

Using Incentives to Motivate Compliance With Responsibilities

As I explained in Chapter 5, if a task is clear, basic, and the child is *response-able*, then incentives or rewards can improve compliance by promoting a tie-in to performance. If you find that your child is having trouble carrying out some of her responsibilities, then you may want to pick one or two to provide incentives for to help her develop a habit. Many parents have tried sticker charts and other such tools and found them to be ineffective. Often, this is because the system is too complicated and includes too many tasks.

If you want to provide an incentive, discuss with your child how and when she can earn a reward. Have her be responsible to you to keep track of her progress, and be willing to be timely in providing her with the reward she has earned. Never forget that your continued praise (remember: *Name, Notice, Nurture*) will be a vital part in motivating her compliance, regardless of any incentive program.

Keeping Track of Incentive Programs

Keep it simple!

Be very clear and specific about your expectations and how the potential reward may be earned. Remember, incentives are to be used for task compliance, not behavior. Especially during the beginning, be willing to help your child succeed, and, if necessary provide a reminder. However, don't provide reminders for too long or too often or they will not need (and have no opportunity to develop) their own way of remembering.

To keep track of the earnings, there are several methods you can use. You can use stickers, marbles, or coins, and there are even apps for smart phones. Try when possible to have a visual reminder of what they are working toward. You can even place dots around the picture to represent their progress as a dot-to-dot that when completed earns them the item pictured. When you award points, always provide ample praise and encouragement. Your smile and kind words really matter.

Once points are earned, they should NOT be taken away. They have been earned for a job done. You may want to consider bonus points if the task is completed especially well or in an especially timely fashion.

One final comment: *Always* be discreet! You don't need to expose your child's program to outsiders. This can be embarrassing for your child and make him less likely to want to participate.

Short, Immediate Rewards for Behavior

If you find that shopping or other errands can be a stressful, wearing experience, especially with younger children, you may want to try a very short, specific incentive program for that event. For example, at the mall, predetermine what your child can get as a reward for good behavior (not wandering, whining, begging, etc.). Be very specific. For each 10 minutes of good behavior, she earns 5 points. She must earn X points to get the reward. If she doesn't earn the reward, she can hold on to those points and use them another time. Try to orchestrate it so that she can earn the reward during the trip to the mall. This will help her stay focused on her goal and help her get back in line if her behavior starts straying.

Tradeoffs between Performance and Behavior

Remember, age is a chronological number—it does not define or dictate readiness or ability. You may see greater improvement and success if you are willing to model for and assist your child a bit longer. She may need your presence to ground her and keep her on task. Be patient and maintain perspective. You may find that the more you push performance, the more stress your child experiences and the harder it becomes for her to regulate her emotions. Sometimes the battles in service of "order and cleanliness" are not worth the strain on the relationship. Adjusting your expectations in one area might allow you to pursue them more fully in other areas.

Are You Trying to Do Too Much?

Some parents, in there efforts to be loving, caring, and wonderful parents, actually do too much – regardless of whether or not their child has ADHD or other challenges. They try to be all things to all people at all times, rarely saying no to requests for help, often sacrificing their own wants, needs and desires in the service of others'. If this sounds like you, consider for a moment the message you are sending out to your family members. While in some ways, it is very loving and caring, you may be giving the impression that other's are not a capable, that others don't need to be as responsible, and that others in your family are more valued than you. As your children grow, you want to make sure they are strong, independent, capable adults who respect you as the same.

Sometimes, it is important to stop a moment and evaluate what you are doing. You may want to leave some space for others in your family to either do more for themselves, or more for you. You may also want to consider modifying or eliminating some of the things you are doing in your efforts to present the best of everything if you find you are having trouble making time for yourself and the other truly important things in your live.

Guiding Thoughts

- Strive to be consistent—but parent the child *you* have!
- To be responsible, you child must be *response-able*.
- Keep it simple and structured when doing reward programs.
- Be clear and explicit regarding your child's rights versus his privileges.
- Be sure you are not trying to be "superparent".

Homework

1. Determine your nonnegotiable house rules. Be clear, concise, and specific.
2. Develop a list of potential incentives with your child. Whenever possible, try to include his participation in the payoff.
3. Discuss with your child what his personal responsibilities are and give him the proper tools to be successful. If necessary, discuss what he needs to help him be successful.
4. Develop a list of what you might be willing to take away from your child if necessary. Keep in mind the potential implications and unintended consequences that might result from the punishment.

ESTABLISH MEANINGFUL CONSEQUENCES

Create Value and Impact

The consequences of an act affect the probability of its occurring again.

—B. F. Skinner

We are now going to be moving into the most challenging part of our parenting work: managing difficult behavior. Up until now we have focused primarily on building your relationship with your child and communicating how you expect her to behave to help her grow into a responsible, respectful, resilient, confident, successful, and independent adult. Many parents who work with me want me to *start* by telling them what consequences they can use to get their kids to actually cooperate and do as they are supposed to do. Unfortunately, as you probably understand by now, there is no easy fix, no easy answer. (So if you have skipped ahead to this chapter, my apologies.)

Having explored how your child's behavior has been impacted by her neurological makeup, her environment, and how you and the other adults in her world communicate with her, we are now ready to add consequences to our home (Figure 7.1).

As you begin to confront the parenting challenges ahead, I

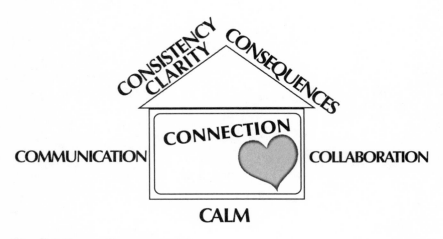

Fig. 7.1 House: Consequences

caution you to carefully monitor, in each situation, your own behavior and attitude. Remind yourself of your knowledge and perspective of your child. Notice for yourself when you are feeling overly anxious or frustrated. Remember, when you lose your calmness, you lose your control. Your child may recognize that in those moments *he* has the power. Step back and regain your composure. What he really needs in those moments is to know that he can count on you for guidance and direction.

Why Are Consequences Necessary?

This may seem like a basic question, but when you stop to really examine it more closely, some of the typical assumptions may come into doubt.

While we may not all agree on the details, most people do agree that one reason societies need consequences to actions is so that they can run smoothly and safely. There are the negative consequences that are given as a result of an action someone takes (such as speeding, vandalizing, or assaulting). There are also negative consequences given as a result of *not* taking an action (such as not paying taxes or registering a motor vehicle). The consequences that are placed upon us as citizens are meant to ensure that individual rights are not violated and that all citizens contribute to our joint society. If there were no laws enforced, our daily lives might be more unstable and perhaps more unsafe.

Parents use consequences as a means of restricting and encouraging certain behaviors as well. Certain consequences are designed to encourage positive behaviors, and others are designed to punish undesirable behaviors. I am going to help you examine how impactful these consequences are for your child and what changes you can introduce to gain a more satisfying result. There is another reason I have found that motivates parents to give consequences, and that is to *guard their kids against potential failure.* In the next chapter, I will explore the impact of consequences when used as a *motivator* for this purpose, but for now, let's begin by exploring more about how consequences can be designed to increase cooperation and reduce noncompliance at home.

Where Do Consequences Come From?

There are five areas of life that can offer consequences to an individual:

1. *Government.* As I mentioned above, there are certain laws that one lives under in any country one is part of. If kids break those laws, while there may be certain leniencies allowed due to age, they are still held responsible for their actions. Generally (when all goes along without corruption), even if a parent disagrees, a child is subject to the law and ruling of the government for the actions he takes.

2. *Society/peers.* As a children age, their parents are less and less able to protect them socially or control the types of relationships that their children develop on their own. How a child interacts with others (his social skills acumen), whether in school, in organized activities, at play dates, or on the playground, will determine how he is treated by society and his peers. Parents can

sometimes change the setting or set the stage, but how the child shows up will help determine the consequences he receives.

3. *Biology*. Regardless of how caring, nice, or bright you may be, no matter how successful you are in certain areas of your life, at the end of the day the consequences for how you feed and treat your body are yours to bear. If you overeat regularly and excessively, you will likely be overweight. If you rarely exercise, you will be less agile and likely more susceptible to various health challenges. Personal hygiene issues are often a big area of concern for parents long before their kids develop awareness of their responsibility for their own teeth, skin, hair, and body odor. And regardless of what parents do or do not do in terms of consequences in this area, life will provide its own.

4. *School*. How kids perform at school, especially as they get older, will determine the consequences they receive in terms of further opportunities within school and the grades they receive. Just as I mentioned above, parents may have limited impact, especially when their kids are young, in terms of influencing the consequences their kids receive for the work that they do. However, each school, just like each government, has its own rules and regulations that determine what happens as a result of kids' actions.

5. *Family*. Here it is—the one area where, as long as a child is not breaking any legal rules, parents have full control as to the consequences they dispense. You get to decide what will happen if your child does or does not do what you ask him or her to do. But as you probably already know, giving consequences and having those consequences be productive and impactful (or even followed) are not always the same thing.

When it comes to the government, society, peers, and biology, we as parents have very little control over the consequences our kids receive. These are, for the most part, *natural consequences*— things that happen in response to our child's behavior without our parental involvement. And, while we can sometimes *change* the school our child goes to, while he is a student of that school our control is limited at best. As parents, we are ultimately most responsible for the *imposed consequences*, those *we* can enforce within our family.

Consequences, no matter where they come from, are effective if they:

- Provide *motivation to prevent* an undesirable behavior from occurring
- Provide *motivation to encourage* a positive behavior to occur
- *Stop* an undesirable behavior while it is happening

What Impact Do Parentally Imposed Consequences Have on Kids?

When life is not giving adequate consequences to kids to change their behavior as parents desire, parents often look to change what would "naturally" occur. Imposed consequences can have the following impact on kids:

- Help kids learn to *delay gratification* for a more valuable future outcome
- Help kids learn to *deal with boring tasks* in service of other needs
- Help kids learn to put the *thoughts and needs of others ahead of their own*

For example, let's say your child usually leaves his backpack on the floor in the kitchen when he comes home from school and immediately goes to the refrigerator for a snack. You have asked him countless times to put his backpack in his room before getting a snack, but to no avail. This would require that he *delay gratification, deal with a boring task,* and put your *thoughts and needs* ahead of his own. If leaving his backpack on the floor does not seem to bother him, generally no "natural" consequence would motivate him to change his behavior in the short term. He needs some other motivation.

When Do Consequences Effectively Motivate People?

So, *motivation* seems to be one important aspect of making a consequence effective. When can the potential imposed consequence motivate a child to comply?

- When he can *anticipate* the impact of his actions
- When he *cares* about the outcome enough to adjust his actions
- When he is *response-able*

Since we know that *kids do well if they can*, then imposed consequences can only work if the child *also* has the skills and tools to go along with the *motivation* to change his behavior.

Punishment Versus Discipline

Before we look more closely at when, why, and how we should impose consequences, I think it is important to think about the language we use in describing our purpose.

- *Punishment* is defined as "retribution for an offense." Punishment is an imposition of an undesirable outcome upon another person and serves to *reinforce who is in control* (the giver of the punishment). Very often, punishment is given *spontaneously* and *without forethought* because of parental frustration and despair. Have you ever found yourself irritated with something your child did and said something you knew was either too extreme or unenforceable? These types of comments generally serve to *erode connection* with your child and her trust in your word and judgment, and may trigger more challenging behaviors than they correct. This is not to say that it is never appropriate or beneficial to impose restrictions or penalties; rather, I want to highlight that when parents announce the consequences for behavior *reactively* and *without prior thought or planning*, the results may be detrimental.

- *Discipline* is defined as "the practice of training people to obey rules or a code of behavior." Discipline is planned *proactively* and based on a set of *predetermined* rules and expectations. The purpose is to *teach the person to use self-control* and responsibility, as she will be held accountable for her actions and decisions. By knowing what to expect beforehand, the child can *develop trust in the integrity of her parent's words and actions*. While she may not always be pleased with her parents for following through with the discipline, she knows in advance what to expect, and the anger and frustration she experiences are more connected to herself than to the discipliner. Discipline is something you do *for* your child, not *to* your child.

What Else Makes a Consequence Effective?

Keep in mind that our goal is to help our kids develop self-regulation and build their *executive function* skills by learning to use their minds to anticipate, plan, and execute their actions with forethought and intention. This requires that they be able to stop, pause, think, and make a better choice *now* for their future. Remember a quote from Dr. Barkley that I introduced in Key 1: "The arguing, defiance, refusal is a learned behavior—not genetic, not biological . . ." He goes on to say, ". . . the child is learning is how to use negative emotion to coerce another into doing what they want, usually leaving them alone." Parents must be strong in their resolve in order to not be shifted from their own position.

Caution is warranted here, though; consequences that are particularly harsh may have your child focusing more on his anger at you than the lessons you are trying to teach. Consequences should point toward the expected behavior as much as possible. They should not just be punitive. The goal is to teach your child what he should do and have him do it.

I like to say that you don't want to "bend the universe" so that kids know what to expect in the real world for their behaviors. When they truly understand the potential impact of their actions, we need to let life teach its lessons. This will be much easier when you are *proactive* in establishing and communicating what your *rules, expectations,* and *consequences* are for his behavior.

When you are giving a preplanned consequence for an undesirable behavior, it is important that you keep in mind the timing and duration of the consequence. Generally, you want your consequence to be as "natural" as possible. It should "fit the crime." For instance, if your child were playing with a ball inappropriately (as you had talked about in advance of giving the ball to your child), taking away the ball would be a logical consequence. And, especially since for kids with ADHD "time is now and not now," it is best to administer the consequence as immediately as possible. This is even more important for younger children, who have so little sense of future time; however, even for older kids and teens, you want consequences to be felt as close to "now" as possible — not the party they may have to miss five days from now. Always keep in mind that it's not necessarily the severity of the consequence that gives it the most impact, but its potential *effect on present and future actions.* The potential of an earlier bedtime tonight may be more impactful than missing a play date four days from now.

As always, you must keep in mind that you need to *"parent the child you have."* As I mentioned very early on, you must keep a *"disability perspective."* Remember that your child may have delays in his development and other factors that make his compliance more challenging. If your child has a difficult time managing his impulsivity, giving him a consequence every time is not necessarily going to prevent his impulsive behavior — it's part of his ADHD makeup. So if your child spontaneously does something (e.g., bounce the ball in the house while waiting for a friend to be ready) and recognizes immediately that he made a mistake, while you might acknowledge the behavior, you don't necessarily need to provide an additional consequence—his self-awareness and remorse may be sufficient lessons. Which is why I add to my previous statement: "Don't bend the universe—*too much*." We do need to let life teach lessons, but along with our cushioning and support as our kids are learning and developing.

When Are We Able to Give Effective Consequences?

As you look back over the parts of the home (Figure 7.1) that we have been building, you see how each of the components of the house are vital in bringing you to a place where you are able to impose effective consequences:

- You must be *calm* enough to think and act on predetermined rules, expectations, and consequences. Remember: Your calm is your power.
- You must have a loving *connection* built on compassion and acceptance of who your child is and what she is capable of.
- You must have the *communication* skills necessary to measure *what* you say and *how* you say your words.
- You must use the tools of *collaborative problem solving* to understand and communicate each other's concerns and perspectives. Make sure that you are clear on your child's concerns and that she really understands why the rule matters to you.
- You must have *clear* and *consistent* rules and expectations. It helps to write down certain rules that are either new or not always followed.
- You must have knowledge about your child's skills and abilities as they relate to her ability to do what is expected of her in the moment of the expectation—you must know he is *response-able*.

Stay strong and confident in the "*black belt*" training you have been participating in so far.

Introducing Negative Consequences

In Key 6, I referred to introducing incentives to help motivate compliance with basic responsibilities. These are rewards you are giving for when your child complies with your expectation. Sometimes, the incentive may not be sufficient to motivate your child to do what he is *able* to do. If you have determined that there will be a penalty for noncompliance, it is often best to have a "training period" or "grace period" set in advance. For example, let's say you discussed the issue of taking dishes out of the bedroom after having a snack. You agreed that if your child forgets to clean up, then the next day he can't have a snack in his room. For the first week, if you notice that your child does not comply, you simply remind him and warn him that next week the penalty will be loss of that privilege for a day. This will give you both time to assess whether the plan is workable and if your child is response-able. Remember, you are looking to build skills, not just gain compliance.

Areas for Giving Imposed Consequences

There are three different areas for developing impactful, effective consequences, and we will explore each one separately:

1. Consequences for disrespecting members of the *family* or the *family values*
2. Consequences for not contributing to the *family* or *home*
3. Consequences for *poor performance* in school or other mandatory activities

At this point, you should have clearly defined your rules and expectations. Take your time and make sure you and your partner truly agree with one another as to what you are willing to enforce, what you want to be working on, and how you will support one another in front of your children if you have disagreements.

1. Consequences for Not Respecting Family Members and Family Values

It is natural to have disagreements, but once the words, body language, and volume get out of hand, things can turn ugly quickly. But, in addition to all the stress and tension that can occur, very often a conversation can turn from emotional disagreement to personal confrontation, where it is not just the issue you are fighting about but personal character.

Respectful communication sets the tone for all that happens. It colors our willingness to listen, respond, compromise, and cooperate. We know that without calm, no learning takes place and no problems are solved. This is not an area in life where you can tell your kids, "Do as I say, not as I do." How you speak, as we have explored, can really impact what happens next. However, as many parents have experienced, *no matter how calm, respectful, and considerate you may be, sometimes your own child can come back at you as someone who is rude, inconsiderate, and simply disrespectful!*

Some parents may choose to ignore this behavior, hoping that somehow it will go away. Generally, this strategy is ineffective. It can lead to giving your child the false impression that somehow either he is justified in his actions or that you are incapable of stopping him because he is more powerful than you are. This can be very dangerous to your relationship, especially as your child grows and the issues you are dealing with become more significant. As I mentioned earlier, all kids need to feel safe, loved, and protected in their home and by their caretakers. They will not feel they can lean on someone they view as emotionally weaker than they are.

There are also parents who feel that they must fight fire with fire. They believe that whatever attitude, volume, or intensity comes at them from their child, they must, as parents, not only match it but also exceed it. Logic might say that this will teach a child that perhaps it's not worth being so tough and the child might back down. There are some kids who do back down, but often the relationship between child and parent suffers and the line of communication is not very productive. Many other kids will not back down from such a battle and the intensity may continue to escalate or simply pick up from the same level each time there is a problem.

A stern, calm, measured, preplanned response is the most effective way of addressing a child who is speaking or acting disrespectfully to a parent. Sometimes, how people express themselves is really their smoke and mirrors to distract from exposing their *anxiety, lack of confidence/comfort,* or *fight for control.* Your child may be communicating *inappropriately*; however, you still need to work hard to *hear* his message. It is important to separate out *what* is said from *how* it is said. You must be clear:

1. The rules for respectful communication do not change based on your mood, feelings, opinion, or the situation.
2. You, as the parent, will not entertain changing your expectation or decision unless and until your child's method of communication has been addressed.

Time Stops

When necessary, you may need to establish a *"time stops"* policy. This is where you, as the parent, stop contributing to your child until such time as a predetermined condition is met. This means that until your child can speak appropriately or do as she has been asked to do:

- There are *no privileges.*
- You will provide *no help or assistance* (including making dinner, driving anywhere, helping with an assignment) except where essential to create calm or ensure safety.

I recommend that you have the specific rules and policies for when *time stops* written out in advance. If your child does not respect this condition, then implement a predetermined consequence.

A helpful way of teaching your child how you will handle these difficult situations is to introduce these steps at a time when there is no conflict:

- *Reflect* back to your child what your child *did* or *said*—what you *saw*, what you *heard* (the behavior).
- *Review* what you believe your child's *concern* and/or her *unexpressed emotion* was (the feeling). Do not at this time answer her demand or offer a solution to her concern. You might perhaps model for her *how she could* express her concern more appropriately.
- *Redo.* Give your child a chance to try again—maybe say what she wants to in an appropriate voice, make a request rather than making a demand, do what she should have done. Sometimes it just takes getting your child to *pause* and notice her own behavior.
- *Respond.* Once your child has adjusted her attitude, presentation, or action, then you can discuss her concern, answer her question, or offer suggestions to help.

Examples:

1. "You are arguing with me about getting dressed for the party. Maybe you are not happy with what we bought. Perhaps it doesn't feel right for some reason, I don't know. Speak to me appropriately and perhaps we can figure this out."
2. "You pushed your food away and made a mess. Maybe you don't like what I made. However, this will not solve the problem."
3. "You just yelled at your sister about switching the TV channel. You may be upset that she has the control; however, that is not how you handle this type of problem."

Use a calm but stern voice. Your child may need a few moments to calm down and perhaps manage her anxiety before she is ready to *redo*. Remember to allow for (and perhaps suggest) a break to let the tension subside. If you do choose to have a conversation, do not focus on what feelings your child was having that led to the conflict and misbehavior. This may cause your child to rationalize her behavior. Often this leads kids to blame some outside person or force as the reason they acted inappropriately. Remind your child that *there is no justification for inappropriate behavior.*

Sometimes in the heat of the moment, it can be difficult to calm yourself and plan what you want to say or do. You want to be careful not to get into a power struggle (remember, you don't want to "raise your hand up the bat"). If possible, announce that you need a moment to calm yourself and decide how you want to respond.

- "Just because you have a need to know now does not mean I have no rights here to think about my answer."
- "Just because you yell does not mean I will do as you wish."
- "I don't like how you responded when I said no."

You might then walk away temporarily, letting your child know that you will return shortly with your response.

If your anticipate that your child might follow you if your were to walk away, then discuss in advance, at a clam, unrelated time, why you might choose to walk away and what your expectation is if you do. If your child follows you, have a *predetermined consequence* for that behavior and give the warning of what that will be. Often, your continued presence facilitates the continued escalation of the negative behavior. Separation from you will give your child a chance to cool down and think rationally. If your child continues to follow, becomes aggressive, and/or threatens damage, you may need to consider leaving the house. Do not do this as a sudden punishment or without a well-thought-out plan. If this is an issue you anticipate, consider making arrangements in advance with a local friend or relative who might be willing to come to your home while you leave for a short time to allow things to cool off.

Making Amends and Rebuilding Trust

Loving, connected relationships are built on *integrity* and *trust*. When there has been a break in the respect, either through words or deeds, this must be acknowledged and repaired. Even though your child may have lost a privilege or opportunity because of his behavior, this may not be enough to rebalance the relationship. There sometimes needs to be a *positive action* the child can do to make up for his misdeed.

For example, let's say Amanda intentionally wrecked the structure that Damien was carefully building. Since this was something she had done in the past and had been warned against, she was asked to leave the playroom as had been discussed previously. That may help reinforce how her actions will be regarded, but how does this help Damien, who just lost 20 minutes of his time working on the building that was wrecked? Perhaps Amanda must now do 20 minutes of Damien's chores, freeing Damien to do as he pleases.

If your child plays ball in the house (against established rules) and accidently brakes your vase, perhaps in addition to losing use of the ball he can make amends to you for his actions. He can certainly clean up the mess (or help you as is age appropriate to do) and maybe either pay some of the monetary value or "pay" though deeds for you. Either way, I encourage you to think not just about *negative consequences* but also *making amends through positive actions*. You may want to consider putting the *positive action* in writing and telling your child that *"time stops"* until he has made amends or at least established what he will be doing to make amends.

While you are having the discussion about what your child did wrong, be sure to focus on the *behavior* as the problem, not the *feeling*. We are all entitled to our feelings, and our feelings are real for each of us. However, negative feelings are no excuse for negative behavior. If you do discuss the feeling that led to the behavior, be sure to talk about other tools or strategies your child has to express his negative feelings rather than the *behavior* he chose to use. For example, you might say, "Next time you are angry at your brother, what can you do?" You may also, if appropriate, help your child see other possible explanations for what he is experiencing. Perhaps Amanda was angry with Damien for using some blocks she had put aside, but Damien didn't know she had done so. Next time, Amanda can ask *why* Damien used those blocks.

Family Service Cards

There may be times when you want your child to do a *positive action* rather than imposing a negative consequence. Keep a list or stack of cards of chores or tasks that your child can do to either help you or the household. Determine the estimated time involved for each item. Depending on your child's age, you can have some tasks that take 10 minutes, some that take 20 minutes, and so forth. When challenging behavior or noncompliance occurs, either tell your child the task or have her pick one from the list or stack of cards for the amount of time you choose.

10-minute tasks	*20-minute tasks*
Sweep the kitchen floor	Clean refrigerator shelves
Bring down/start laundry	Fold laundry
Organize pantry shelves	Do a sibling's chore

2. Consequences for Not Contributing to the Family or Home

It's very frustrating for some parents when they feel that with all they do for their kids, their kids seem resistant or oblivious to helping contribute to the home when they are asked. This can be anything from the chores that have been assigned, to helping out when requested (such as unloading groceries from the car or getting a jar of tomato sauce from the pantry).

I have said throughout that *"kids do well if they can,"* and yet it still seems there are times when they *can* but *don't* do as they should. Remember, there are still many reasons kids with ADHD will not be doing what they can.

- Time is now and not now
- They have a harder time delaying gratification
- They have difficulty putting on the brakes and transitioning

And sometimes the problem is that they are not connecting the impact of their present actions with their future opportunities or relationships.

I discussed in Key 6 the importance of choosing some responsibilities that your child should have to help make sure she is able to comply with your requests and contribute to your home. Remember that it is important to be clear, for yourself and for your child, whether the thing you are asking her to do is a *preference* or an *obligation*. There is a big difference in how you communicate your *request* that Nora help you unload the car versus your *expectation* that she do so. If it is simply a request, then you are genuinely open to her saying no; perhaps she is busy with something or really tired from her day. However, if it is an expectation, then even if she is busy or tired, you expect her to comply. If this is the case, *say what you mean and mean what you say.*

Be prepared to enforce your request. But, before you do, ask yourself if your child responded with his objection appropriately and reasonably. His response or explanation may add new insight. Perhaps you need to work together toward a new solution that is mutually acceptable. Your willingness to do so shows your child that you respect her. Remember, the goal is not always *compliance*. Sometimes, it's behavioral improvement if Liam pauses and responds calmly, respectfully, and considerately when he objects. You may gain more by praising his actions than by having him help with the groceries in that moment.

If you still feel that Liam should be doing, as you asked, then make sure you have set up in advance what will happen if he *does not meet your expectation.* In Key 6, you may have chosen one or two specific actions that you were providing incentives for. As I mentioned earlier in this chapter, you may want to have a "training period" and then be prepared with a predetermined consequence for noncompliance. Have the consequence clearly defined, discussed (perhaps a "Plan B" conversation to ensure that your child has contributed his concerns, ideas, etc.), and perhaps written down as a mini-contract. It may feel uncomfortable to have a formal agreement with your child; however, the battles and hardship it can prevent will pay off for all as you create more calm, compliance, and independence in your home. Keep in mind that the primary purpose of developing a written contract is to be sure there is no misunderstanding as to the rules, responsibilities, privileges, and consequences established in your home. By proactively addressing areas of concern, you will be reducing the opportunity for miscommunication, inconsistency, and the careless use of punishment. This contract must be discussed with and signed by each person who will be responsible for its fulfillment: parents, significant caregivers, and children/teens.

Sample Contract

You are responsible to take out the garbage on Monday and Thursday evenings by 5:30 p.m. If you are not home at this time, you must do it within 30 minutes of being home.

Privilege: Each day that you remember without any reminder, you earn $1.

Consequence: You may have no food, screen time, phone, music, or social time and your door must remain open until this chore is complete.

No one likes to be the "nag. So let your plan do the speaking. Point to the paper or chart and be prepared to follow through. Remember, you *will not* allow yourself to get swayed by your child's anger, frustration, or unhappiness. He *can* learn to deal with his feelings and regulate his emotions if what you have asked him to do is reasonable. He may test you at first. Remember, some kids, especially the strong-willed ones, will try to renegotiate, talk you out of your concerns, or even try to tell you that you are being unreasonable or worse. Trust your gut and stand your ground. This is the only way change will happen.

When Things Go Wrong

As much as you may try and your child may try, *this is not easy.* True change does take time (some say thirty to forty times, or two to four months of consistency). Be patient with yourself. Remember some of these guidelines:

- Remain calm. Pause and be willing to stop to think.
- Be sure your child truly understood/heard what you said.
- No arguing, no negotiating, no reacting unless your child speaks appropriately.
- Talk little, emote less. Simply restate the rules and the consequences.
- Remind him "the choice is yours" and be sure he is clear on his choices.
- Maybe he just needs a chance to "chill" before moving forward.
- You must be willing to "turn the car around" or leave even if it means you don't get to do what you wanted to do.
- Remain calm. Yes, I am repeating myself.
- Don't always take their behavior personally—it's not always about you.

And after there has been a stressful situation, be willing to move on and let it go. Reconnect and forgive. Offer a hug or some reassuring words; this is not the time for a lecture. It's all about empathy. Your child did not choose to be difficult—who would? Don't let the difficulty blind you to her wonderful characteristics. Imagine for just one moment what intense, negative thoughts and emotions your child is experiencing during difficult explosions. Anger? Anxiety? Alone? Rejected? Embarrassed? Stupid? Scared? Perhaps for just one moment you can remove your own reactions and judgments about how your child "should" be behaving and recognize that this is, in this moment, a child in distress. How you respond can act to escalate or deescalate the situation. You already know where escalation can bring you. It is only in a place of calm where learning, growth, and positive resolution can occur.

3. Consequences for Poor Performance in School or Other Mandatory Activities

Parents and teachers sometimes see a child's inactivity, avoidance, or rushed work and assume that "he's just not motivated." The truth is, he *is* motivated, but perhaps not in a positive direction. He may be motivated to resist, avoid, and sometimes just to retain some control over his life. It helps to recognize that these children are not helpless victims; they are unskilled and/or unable to solve their problems in an effective way.

Before I speak about ways to handle situations where kids do not perform up to their potential or expectations in school or in other mandatory activities (as determined by parents, such as religious school, musical instruments, sports), let's take a moment and be the child in school. For some kids, whether explicitly or implicitly, they hear certain messages all day long:

- Sit still
- Do it "my way"
- Work longer
- Deal with your boredom
- Try harder
- Care more
- Focus harder, longer
- Hurry up

And here is what they may be dealing with in their brain as they are in school:

- Deficits in working memory
- Slower processing speed
- Stifled creative energy
- Limited time, resources, or opportunity to explore interests
- Limited time (and sometimes skill) for socializing
- Boundless energy they must contain
- Underactive neurotransmitters when bored
- Delays and deficits in executive function skills

I had a client a few years ago who showed me her son's doodle from his seventh-grade math notebook. There, alongside his notes and calculations, he had drawn a picture that to me spoke so clearly. He drew a large funnel labeled "Average Brain" and a small funnel labeled "ADHD Brain." Next to these funnels he drew a teacher speaking lots of letters and a boy (himself) with a small funnel on his head. Some of the letters were inside the funnel and some fell outside the funnel. His comment: "School s—ks. Some things just don't fit." He was painfully aware that he just couldn't keep up with the pace of the class, even though he was a very intelligent boy.

Sometimes kids deserve credit for just showing up at school!

What Role Should Parents Play With Regard to Their Involvement With School?

So when it comes to school, what is a parent to do? Parents sometimes grapple with knowing when and how to pull back support and supervision, or when they must become firmer in their expectations and involvement. There are the academic concerns (does your child *understand* the material?), but there are also the *executive function* skills concerns—time management; organization; regulating attention, effort, processing speed, and emotions to stay with doing all the work—that are often the most pressing for kids with ADHD.

If your child is struggling with the material itself, it is important to rule out any learning disabilities (which frequently coexist with ADHD). Perhaps some additional tutoring or extra help at school is warranted.

If your child is struggling to manage because of his *executive function* deficits and you are helping manage the homework process, make sure that the teacher is aware of the role you are playing and that you work collaboratively with the teacher. It is important that the teacher knows how much help and support you are providing so that she has a realistic view of your child's skills. Remember, you want to help develop skills, not dependence, so it is important that you are all working together. Unfortunately, there are some teachers who may feel that parents are overinvolved in their child's work, not recognizing or knowing the true impact of ADHD and executive function deficits on learning and performing. If you are in that situation, I urge you to provide your teacher with information, perhaps excerpts from this book or articles on my website. If necessary, persist beyond the teacher to the special education department or school principal. Training in ADHD and *executive function* skills is sometimes necessary for school personnel. A list of accommodations and modifications the school can provide is given in Appendix C.

The question of your involvement, beyond academic support and minimal assistance with managing the homework process, will often depend on your child and your relationship. Does he perceive your help and guidance as motivating and supportive, or is he resisting your efforts as intrusive, nagging, or controlling? If your child is okay with you being involved, then you will want to be cautious as to *how* involved you become. Sometimes parents help their kids beyond what a teacher might expect when it comes to completing homework, studying, and projects. In an effort to help their struggling child, some parents help complete homework the child should have completed independently so that he is not marked down for handing it in with errors or late. Or a parent may take the "team" approach for projects. I have often heard parents talk about how "we" have so much homework, or how "we" have to work on "our" project.

It is important for both your child and you to find the balance between support and enabling, between realistic expectations and necessary modifications. My definition of enabling is this: Any actions taken for or on behalf of your child that postpone or prevent him from experiencing the natural consequences of his actions, decisions, or behaviors that he would receive in the outside world—on an ongoing basis. When you allow your child to feel the true impact of his decisions, he will be faced with the true experience of the effects of these decisions. Perhaps then he may be forced to make the hard choice to either accept his lot or work in true partnership to change it.

Collaborating with your child and his teachers about the role you play can be helpful in terms of transparency and being able to provide valuable support. If necessary, reach out to other school personnel for added input.

The real dilemma that comes up for some parents is, "If I back off, he might . . . *fail.*" There is *no easy answer,* but we will explore this issue in depth here and in the next chapter.

Imposing Consequences for School Performance

If your child does push back when you offer—or insist on providing—support, then what role should imposed consequences play when it comes to doing homework, projects, and grading performance?

When I wrote earlier about the impact parent-imposed consequences have on kids, I mentioned that imposed consequences can help kids learn to:

- Delay gratification for a more valuable future outcome
- Deal with boring tasks in service of other needs
- Put the thoughts and needs of others ahead of their own

However, for kids who struggle with flexibility, frustration tolerance, and adaptability, *and* for kids who are very focused on being independent, parent-imposed consequences can sometimes:

- Shut kids down (remember the impact of stress and pressure)
- Increase their anxiety and feelings of shame
- Erode their self-confidence
- Damage their trust and connection with others
- Cause them to focus more on *defying to survive* than on *learning to grow*

When a child views the expectations placed on him as unreasonable, he often views the person assigning those expectations as threatening, unreasonable or worse. And when this person is the parent he loves, trusts, and wants to please, the child can be in conflict between his *thinking brain*, which tells him that he *should* do what is expected, and his *emotional brain*, which tells him that he *can't*. He speaks a big, convincing story about how he wants to, and he can, and he will, because he knows it's the right thing to say and it is what is expected. But inside, there is a part of him that feels he cannot. This is when you start to see "magical thinking" ("Of course I will get it done"), "bravado" ("I can handle all this; I don't need help"), and the fight, flight, or freeze response.

"I Don't Want You to Be So Involved"

If this sounds like your child, take a step back and see what changes need to be made. Seeing your child, who is bright and capable, *not* doing as she should can be very frustrating and painful for all concerned. Simply adding additional controls and consequences is more likely to widen the emotional gap between you and your child and increase her resistance than it is to help her change her ways and perform as she should. Perhaps she needs adjustments in her academic program, or perhaps she needs support to see her skills more positively than she does, or perhaps she suffers from some anxiety or depression that is not allowing her to face her challenges.

However, some kids just *do not want the help that is offered by their parents*. In fact, some kids don't want Mom and Dad anywhere near their work! For some kids, this happens much earlier than would seem reasonable or even appropriate; it's just part of their strong-willed character. For other kids, as they progress into their teen years, this is part of a healthy progression toward independence—even if their skills do not match their age. Imposed consequences may get certain things accomplished in the short term, but they will not aid this natural internal process toward independence along if the child's *focus* is on fighting for control and pushing away the involvement of others.

So how do you "help" if your child is resisting? What consequences *should* you impose?

To be continued with Key 8: Choices.

Guiding Thoughts

- Although negative consequences may stop negative behavior, positive consequences are the best way to encourage positive behavior.
- We cannot control our children's behavior, but we can give clear messages as to what we expect and will accept.
- Be willing sometimes to give extra chances and praise to counteract the negative messages from the outside world.
- Plan ahead and anticipate trouble spots.
- Look for conversations, not confrontations.
- Act, don't yak! Give clear choices and hold the lecture.
- Do not bend the universe—too much!
- Do not always take their behavior personally. Stay strong.
- Requiring a positive action rather than taking something away can teach a more powerful lesson.
- Reflect, Review, Redo, Respond.

- Be willing to walk away for now.
- No lectures when it's over. Reconnect as soon as possible.

Homework

1. Determine one or two responsibilities where you want to improve your child's compliance. Once you have had a week or so where you and your child know what is expected and your child has had an opportunity to succeed with support (and possibly a reward), introduce the consequence for when she does not comply. If necessary, set up a written contract for a responsibility you wish to reinforce.
2. Develop a list of chores or tasks your child can do in case she is disrespectful or noncompliant. Have a variety of tasks, both quick ones and more involved ones.
3. Clearly write down what the rules are for when *"time stops."*
4. If you child tends to follow you when you try to walk away, have a discussion about that concern and make a plan and possible consequence if she is unable to separate from you properly.

KEY 8

CHOICES

Yours and Theirs

In the long run, we shape our lives, and we shape ourselves.
The process never ends until we die. And the choices we make
are ultimately our own responsibility.

—Eleanor Roosevelt

So now, having learned how ADHD truly impacts your child's life, and having seen the importance of Calm, Connection, Communication, Collaboration, Clarity, Consistency, and Consequences, the greatest lesson left to be learned is Choices—what choices to give them, and equally important, *how to personally handle the choices that they make.* This is the final piece of the house (Figure 8.1).

At this point, I have laid out very specific, rational steps for being clear, consistent, and proactive in setting boundaries and expectations for your kids. I have provided you with guidance for communicating and collaborating as much as possible to ensure that both your and your child's concerns are understood and met, as well as guidelines for when they do not meet your expectations within your family life.

I ended the previous chapter introducing the issue of *imposed consequences* in the area of school and other parent-directed mandatory activities (religious school, music instruments, sports, etc.).

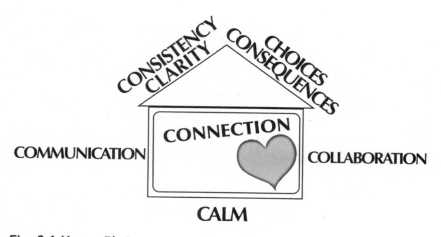

Fig. 8.1 House: Choices

This is an area of stress for so many families. Some kids with ADHD, even in the early years of school when many of their peers are just coasting along with the homework, find school and homework to be so stressful and challenging that it spills over into other aspects of life. They may not yet have even developed an understanding of the reasons for the true challenges they are facing.

Remember that *kids do well if they can.* The challenges kids with ADHD face are real and can greatly impact their learning. For kids with ADHD and *executive function* challenges, extra guidance, structure, and support not only are beneficial in helping them develop their *executive function* skills and helping them to be more productive and successful students, but they are essential and *should be required.* While fortunately there are some schools that recognize this and are working toward providing the proper support, there are many kids who are expected to adapt as best they can, while still being held accountable to the same standard. It reminds me of my experience as a child in gym class. The teacher was teaching everyone how to hold a tennis racket and hit a serve. "Lefties, just do the opposite." I never could figure that out.

Parents Must Advocate for Their Kids

If your child is struggling in school, it is sometimes hard to evaluate whether he is getting the proper support for his challenges. I encourage parents that it is *their responsibility* to learn as much as they can about what supports, in school and out of school, their child needs to be successful. As I said in the first chapter of this book, so much of what we have learned about ADHD and *executive function* challenges, we have learned in the past decade. Unfortunately, there are many wonderful, well-meaning teachers, staff members, and administrators who do not know enough about how to help kids manage ADHD and boost their *executive function* skills in the classroom. When I lecture in and consult in schools, I usually find that teachers are very grateful to gain new insights and strategies to help their students.

If you feel that your child is not getting the proper support, here are some steps you can take:

- Keep a notebook with specific observations and accounts that reflect your areas of concerns. For instance, you can include how long it takes you child to do homework; how often he forgets or misplaces materials, forgets to write down assignments, or doesn't understand assignments; or the specific struggles he has in doing the work. Include his accounts of what happens for him during class if he tells you of his struggles there as well.
- If you suspect any learning disabilities or if ADHD has not been formally diagnosed, you can request that your child be evaluated by the school and considered for special education services. (See Appendix D for a letter to request services.)
- Resources such as this book exist to offer education, tools, and strategies all aimed at providing a range of support. Respectfully find a way to convey some of the learning you have acquired about ADHD that you feel would be helpful for your child's teachers to know. Here are some strategies that may help:

◊ Begin the year with a brief, personal description of your child's disability that includes the "softer" points beyond the testing results. How does he best learn? How is he motivated? What are his triggers? What has worked in the past?

◊ Emphasize the importance of discretion and privacy. Discuss specific strategies the teacher utilizes when kids don't listen or are disruptive. Offer your own suggestions if you have additional ideas.

◊ Discuss with your child's teacher, perhaps along with your child if appropriate, how they can work together when things are difficult and not going well. Emphasize that the goal is not punishment; rather, it's to solve problems and gain skills.

As you approach your teacher to discuss your child, keep in mind the following: This is the person who is with your child each and every school day. Empathize with the fact that he or she is responsible for managing and supporting not just your child, but also a whole classroom of students. Even if you suspect otherwise, approach teachers with the attitude that they want to help and that you value their insights. However, although they may have the best intentions, they may not yet understand how to help your child, and in fact may be unknowingly frustrating and alienating and perhaps even harming your child. If repeated experience with a given teacher leads you to conclude that he or she is not supportive of your efforts to collaborate, then you may want to involve the guidance counselor or school principal.

What About the Kids Who Strongly Resist Help?

If you have a child who strongly resists your and others' involvement, you need to evaluate *why she is so resistant*. As I mentioned in the previous chapter, you want to be sure to assess whether the academic program is appropriate. You also want to consider whether your child is dealing with anxiety or depression that makes him want to push off the added pressure of school.

About the Academic Program and Extracurricular Activities

These days, with the added competition and pressure kids are under to qualify for admission to colleges and universities, as well as added pressures on high schools to show that they are offering top-level classes, more and more kids are feeling pressure from their parents, their peers, and their schools to take Advanced Placement (AP) and/or International Baccalaureate (IB) courses. Additionally, many kids feel similar pressure to become very involved in extracurricular activities for the purpose of developing a stellar resume for college applications.

While these courses and activities are appropriate and reasonable for some kids, there are many kids (with ADHD and without) who are working beyond what they can reasonably manage well. The level of pressure they are under is impacting them developmentally by providing them little time to exercise, sleep, or spend important time with family or friends. Not to mention the impact we know stress has on learning!

It is especially important (and understandably frustrating) for kids with ADHD (and their parents) to recognize that while they may be *academically qualified* for certain AP/IB classes, because of the extra time they need for reading, studying, and projects, they may not be able to keep up—or may do so at the expense of other courses or obligations. These are still important growing years. I encourage all parents to recognize, and help their kids recognize, that there are an abundance of excellent college and post high school programs available. You want your child to not just get into the next program, but *be able to thrive there* as well. The tradeoff of taking certain AP/IB classes may be that the child cannot excel in multiple areas of her current life as a result of needing to spend too much time on these specific classes. I explain this concept to parents and teachers with this analogy:

Let's assume you have $1 to spend on grades in your academic courses. In terms of time and effort, it would cost you the following to get a B+ or higher in each class:

Math: 20¢
A/P Social Studies: 40¢ (you struggle with all the reading)
Science: 10¢ (your passion)
Spanish: 30¢
English: 20¢

Clearly, if the child had more money (extra time) she might be able to succeed at all these subjects. Instead, to keep up with the goal or expectation, time is often taken away from sleep, food, exercise, or other developmentally valuable activities. Be prepared in advance so you can *each* set *reasonable expectations*.

In addition to the kids who are resisting your involvement for the reasons I just mentioned, there are some kids who are, as I said in Key 2, like *cactus flowers*—they will not be rushed to bloom and will open at their own rate. I have worked with many families of kids who, well before their age and knowledge may dictate, are determined to chart their own course, make their own decisions, and learn life's lessons on their own terms. They are the daredevils, or the trailblazers, and, as I call them, the *strong-willed* kids. They will test your instincts and your resolve. They can leave you shaking your head and wondering why they want to take a more difficult road of independence when there are so many around them ready, willing, and wanting to help. For some of these kids, especially as they get older, you may need to pull back your involvement more than your gut wants you to. Which leads to the inevitable quandary: *But if I back off, he might . . . fail!*

A Word About the Histories of Some Strong-Willed Kids

In the 1998 Apple computer ad *Think Different*, several illustrious, successful people, many known or assumed to have ADHD (such as Ted Turner, Sir Richard Branson, Jim Henson, and Albert Einstein) were shown on-screen as the following words played:

Here's to the crazy ones.
The misfits.
The rebels.
The troublemakers.
The round pegs in the square holes.
The ones who see things differently.
They're not fond of rules.
And they have no respect for the status quo.

You can quote them, disagree with them, glorify or vilify them.
About the only thing you can't do is ignore them.

Because they change things.
They push the human race forward.
While some see them as the crazy ones, we see genius.

Because the people who are crazy enough to think they can
change the world, are the ones who do.

Before we look more closely at how to handle the kids who resist parental involvement, I want to just revisit our initial role and our goal as parents.

What Is Our Role as Parents?

As much as we would all love to see our kids happy and successful, we know that this is not something we can control. As parents, we can provide them a variety of opportunities. We should also provide them with tools, strategies, and supports to help them develop their *executive function* skills. We can also help build their confidence and give them a strong sense of themselves by praising them fully—letting them know *what* they are doing well and how valuable that is (remember, *Notice, Name,* and *Nurture*). Reminding them of what you *like* about them is a very powerful reinforcer—

and don't limit this to behavior. For example, saying, "Wow, you have really gotten into learning about old cars. I like the way you pursue your passion" can help your child feel respected for his interests and valued for his persistence and inquisitiveness, and can open the door for you to help him see how these traits can transfer to other challenges and opportunities.

I encourage you to be patient and tolerate a possibly greater need to be involved as your child's assistant *executive function* CEO as he learns to internalize his own skills. He will need more hands-on parenting, but sometimes with a more subtle delivery. And once you have helped set the foundation, don't be in a rush to back away. You will need to find your way to be there in the background. No judging, no nagging. Be sensitive to his growing sense of self and his pride as you weave back and forth between doing for him, teaching him, and leaving space for him to do it on his own.

You can *offer support* without *giving support*. Before jumping in, ask, "Would you like my help on . . . ?" And especially for teens, who are often reluctant to share with parents but do occasionally let loose with what is on their minds, you might say, "Would you like my input or opinion, or did you just want to share (or vent) about what's going on?" This gives them the space to choose what role they want you to play while still keeping the door open for connection.

As you collaborate to solve problems, remember that even if your child's idea is not the best, letting him *experience* what happens when he tries his plan may still have value if in the process you are both able to communicate and he feels valued and trusted to have a say in decisions concerning himself.

Remember our goal—to help kids develop self-regulation and self-motivation. *Stay in the present—as challenging as the present may be!* Growth is not always visible, but it does happen. Now is your time to plant seeds and not get invested in whether your child chooses to follow your advice in the moment. As Mark Twain said, "When I was a boy of fourteen, my father was so ignorant I could hardly stand to have the old man around. But when I got to be twenty-one, I was astonished by how much he'd learned in seven years."

Keep in mind that it's *not just the academic content* your child needs to be learning. He is working on forming his views and expectations about himself and developing his motivation for his own achievement. As important as academics are, your child's view of himself, his self-worth, his optimistic view of his own future, and his belief that there are caring people in their world who truly understand him and will be supportive of him, are much more important in shaping his future.

But If I Back Off, She Might Fail

This is one of the greatest challenges and concerns many parents face when their child strongly resists their best attempts at guiding and supporting: "Do I tighten the controls to make sure she does as she is supposed to, or do I pull back and let her risk failure, or at a minimum not reach her potential?" There really are a few issues here:

- Fail at what? Remember, there are *many* things kids are learning as students. Academics are clearly important; however, even academics must be seen in balance with all of the child's challenges.
- At whose agenda? Whether parents agree or disagree, the child still has to *choose* to want to learn. I once saw a bumper sticker on a car that read "They can send me to college but they *can't* make me think!" Remember, we can control their external options, but not their internal choices.
- Is she failing? Or is she just not meeting other people's expectations?

Very often parents focus on goals they think are important without regard for the big picture of how the tradeoff involved in reaching these goals may be affecting their child. And sometimes parents become invested in what their children say they want to accomplish or become overly concerned that their kids will miss an opportunity now that will damage their future.

If your child is not being as productive as she "needs" to be, allowing that concern to become an emotional battle may end up creating or exacerbating behavioral problems. In other words, getting angry and punishing may not, in the long run, motivate your child to get her work done and in fact may shut her down and send her deeper into a hole. Think back to what is involved in *motivation*:

- *Autonomy:* The innate desire to be self-directed and have control over one's life.
- *Mastery:* The desire to make progress and improve.
- *Purpose:* The desire to feel we are making a contribution and that we matter.

I encourage you to recognize when there is a power struggle ensuing. You must still be the parent; you must still be present and effective in ensuring that your child is safe, morally appropriate, and setting herself toward a productive future. However, your primary concern in the present might need to shift focus while you create and maintain an atmosphere of calm and reestablish connection. As we discussed before, this must be the foundation and core of your home. Without this, no learning can take place — academically, socially, or emotionally.

Failure Is Sometimes Developmentally Vital and Should Not Always Be Prevented

So many of life's greatest lessons are learned by trial and error. But before one has the opportunity to experience these lessons, one *must have the freedom of choice* to pursue the experience. Choice is power:

- It means you can exercise free will
- It means you have an opportunity to impact the outcome

- It means you have a responsibility
- It also involves *risk* that you might succeed—or might fail.

When you have a child who truly wants you to back off, there are a few different approaches you might take—especially if that child is a teen. However, and most important, I recommend that they each include a *collaborative discussion* and a *written agreement* that includes a specific date to review and evaluate the agreement. First ask yourself: Are you truly willing to give your child the space she is requesting to develop her sense of her own abilities, motivation, and commitment? Are there any limits or boundaries involved in your willingness to extend certain freedoms, and if so, what are they? In essence, you will be communicating to your child that she is the *captain of her ship*. William Ernest Henley ends his inspirational poem "Invictus" with the lines "I am the Master of my fate: I am the Captain of my soul."

Here are a few of the main considerations you will want to cover as you discuss pulling back your involvement:

- What will your role be in terms of direct support? Keep in mind that, especially for kids with ADHD, their focus may not be on their actual work until the "fire is at the door," so to speak. Remember that for them, time is now . . . and not now. So while you may be painfully aware that there is a project due in three days that Libby has not started, part of Libby's request, and now responsibility (and opportunity for learning), is that *she is the one in charge of the planning and doing*. You might want to agree, for example, that even if panic sets in, you are not expected to pull an all-nighter with her or do work for her that she was capable of doing if she had properly planned. This does not mean that you are unwilling to help, simply that her requests must be reasonable and appropriate. The more you can discuss your role in advance, the more you will be helping your child develop her *executive function* skills.

- How long will this agreement last? Especially starting out, you may want to agree to a trial period (depending on your child's age, this could be a few weeks, or until either midway through or at the end of the marking period), as you each get comfortable trusting one another. Your child needs to develop trust that she truly *is in charge*, and that you are truly willing to give her the space she is requesting to develop her sense of her own abilities, motivation, and commitment. You also want to develop trust that she truly wants to be working toward her own progress.

- By setting a specific time to review the agreement, you will have an opportunity to see if adjustments need to be made. You can also hopefully have an opportunity to acknowledge and praise your child's growth and success. You might even suggest that your child reward her *own success* by tracking her progress with some sort of tangible marker or allowing herself some type of treat.

- Keep in mind that the objective is not simply for your child to prove she can get good grades; it is also for her to learn how she is as CEO of her own brain. If she has not fulfilled her agreement, what does she believe has gotten in the way? What does she intend to do differently? Is she showing genuine willingness to make changes moving forward? Remember, revisit a Plan B conversation before going back to Plan A.

- Will there be a "bottom line" level of failure that will trigger your involvement? Every parent has their own level of how much they can tolerate standing back if their child does not perform up to expectations. Keep in mind that, very often, kids also have their own comfort level as well that can naturally push them to make the necessary changes and adjustments when they feel the full weight of their responsibility.

- In your collaboration, ask your child what grade she wants to set as a goal for each class and what grade she thinks she can reasonably earn. You might also include an agreement about what grade will trigger a new discussion and possibly a new intervention. For example, she might say that she wants to earn an A in math and feels that with reasonable effort she should be able to earn at least a B. You may set your threshold at a C before you agree that a new discussion and possibly a new plan is necessary.

- If necessary, you may also include in your agreement a preplanned vehicle for knowing if grades and/or performance dip to a certain level. If necessary or appropriate, you and your child can let the teacher know about the agreement you have both made so that the teacher is aware that there is a plan in place and that you are allowing your child some leeway in your personal involvement.

- As part of your agreement, you may want to offer your child the option of meeting with an *ADHD coach*. (See Appendix A for information about ADHD coaching.) The role of the coach will be to support your child, not to be the enforcer of your personal agenda. Effective coaching can be very powerful in helping a child learn skills and gain awareness about herself, without the emotional layers often involved between parent and child. In other words, the coach is there to help your child succeed in managing her work, learn strategies, and so forth, not to report back to you about what is being accomplished. In order for this to be effective for a resistant child, there has to be trust and transparency that the coach's alliance is with the child, not the parent. You may include in your agreement that the coach must be kept informed by your child of her progress, and will notify you only with your child's prior knowledge if grades or progress have declined to an agreed-upon level. Of course, the coach should first encourage the child to be the one to share this information herself.

Freedom of Choice

Freedom of choice builds pride and self-esteem from knowing that one has ownership and responsibility over what one has accomplished. Failure can be a positive step toward growth if one is given the *opportunity to learn without shame, blame, or criticism.* True growth and confidence will happen as your child takes ownership over himself and his destiny. Having the *freedom to fail* allows kids to develop *naturally* according to their innate gifts, talents, and passions.

Let your child know this:

Conscious Failure, meaning that you *choose your actions knowing the risk you were taking,* means that even though you didn't succeed, you stepped out on your own and took responsibility for your actions.

How powerful, how daring is that!

How impressive that you value yourself enough to try. That you have confidence that you CAN!

Success involves a plan, hard work, effective strategies, persistence, gumption, and a willingness to fail—and a healthy dose of empathy, patience, and tolerance from supportive parents.

I once heard someone say, "It's not the challenges you face but the choices you make in facing those challenges that matters." If failure does occur, focus on the next step forward. Hold the lectures and the "I told you so's," since no doubt your child is painfully aware of his failure already.

But what if your child really *doesn't* care about school?

If the truth is that your child really doesn't care about school right now, maybe it's better to make it safe for him to be truthful and find *some* level of success rather than having him focus his energy on deceit or avoidance. It is better to help kids learn to love learning than to hate all school. They need to see that it is important to *learn how to learn* even if the subject they are learning is not always interesting to them.

Perhaps there is a strong interest and passion that your child is devoted to that he can demonstrate he is committed to learning about and growing with. You may want to collaborate on choosing one or two subjects for now that he will put true energy into, in addition to this outside interest, and accept a lower level of performance on other specific subjects while he invests his energy productively elsewhere. As Mark Twain said, "I never let my schooling get in the way of my education."

In school, kids are expected to be an expert in a variety of areas, but in the real world, if you keep your options open by gaining a good foundation of knowledge and strong life skills, as an adult you can generally pick and choose the areas you focus on based on your skills and interests. Help kids see themselves not just as students, but also as individuals with other aspects to their lives.

School may be really hard for some of these kids, but help them believe that *in life, they will rock!*

Famous Failures

If you or your child needs some comfort or inspiration from seeing other people experience tremendous success after significant failure, here are a few wonderful examples from history:

The Beatles were turned down by Decca Records, who felt that guitar groups were on the way out and that the Beatles had no future in show business.

Michael Jordan was cut from his high school basketball team but went on to win the NBA Championship title with the Chicago Bulls six times.

Thomas Edison was considered a poor student in school and was pulled early on and homeschooled by his mother.

How Are You Doing?

Sometimes parents I work with have needed to recognize that their *own anxiety,* and sometimes their *own dreams for their kids,* has been getting in the way of *"parenting the child they have."* If this is you, you are not alone.

- Make sure you are involved in other aspects of your own life besides your role as parent. Perhaps use the Wheel of Life (see below) to see what other parts of your life needs attention.
- Make sure you are taking care of yourself in terms of your own sleep, exercise, and nutrition.

- Be sure to feed your marriage or relationship with your partner as well as your friendships with the time and effort they deserve so that you don't become isolated or alienated.
- Seek out support from other parents going through similar challenges.
- Consider acknowledging to your child the struggle you are having, while being sure to frame it in a way that builds confidence in their growth and their future. "It's not easy for me to pull back; I've been 'Mom' all these years. But I see you are growing and I have to get used to the changes that are happening. Promise, I'm working on it."

Parents often feel that "the stakes are too big now; I can't let her fail at this point."

- Third grade: "I can't let her fail; it's a turning point when kids are starting to really have to apply themselves."
- Sixth grade: "If I pull back now, he will not succeed and then feel badly about himself—middle school has enough challenges."
- Ninth grade: "It's the beginning of high school. This all matters for her transcript now."
- Eleventh grade: "This is the final push. If he doesn't pull his grades up now, he won't get into a good college."

There is a tremendous and growing problem today where kids who may have flourished during their high school career are not succeeding when they begin college. I often receive phone calls from parents and young adults who are baffled and frustrated as they deal with an unsuccessful foray into college. Parents are surprised and dismayed that their child has been placed on academic probation. Students find themselves woefully unprepared for all that is expected of them in their new role as an independent adult.

There is a video I show during my parent workshop that portrays the story of Ricochet, a dog who learned how to surf and help disabled children after she was released from her "typical" service program (www.surfdogricochet.com). Ricochet had been learning as a puppy how to tend to people with disabilities, but as she grew, "so did her instinct for chasing birds," which could put a person with disabilities at risk. I always think of Ricochet as a dog who has ADHD. Her trainer tried for months to "make" her something she was not, and she was finally released from the program. In the video, her trainer says:

> I was very disappointed. But rather than focus on what she couldn't do, I focused on what she could do—which was surfing. She was a different dog when she surfed . . . totally joyful and 100% committed to her new direction. When I let go of who I wanted her to be and just let her "be," she completely flourished, and I reveled in knowing she is perfect just the way she is.

Without learning the necessary life skills to balance all the different aspects life (studying, socializing, budgeting, laundry, waking up on time, sleeping enough, etc.) and developing their own resources, strategies, and discipline to succeed independently, students often become overwhelmed and are unable to succeed on their own. So when is the right time to let kids experience the weight of their own choices or risk failure? While you are still actively present in their lives to help them learn from their mistakes. As the Ricochet video plays, we can hear Taylor Hick's song "Do I Make You Proud?"

The Wheel of Life

There is a tool we use in coaching, called the Wheel of Life, that visually depicts the various aspects of our lives to help assess how satisfied we are in each area. This is a simple tool that can be adapted for a variety of life's challenges, such as parenting, career, marriage, and being a child. In Figures 8.2 and 8.3 I have included four samples: two for kids and two for parents. You can adapt your circle to represent any concerns you have. This is an excellent tool for facilitating a conversation about where your child is feeling confident, successful, or satisfied and where he may need some

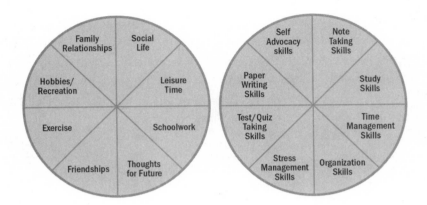

Fig. 8.2 Wheel of Life for Students

strengthening, perhaps with support or guidance. And along the way, you may see the areas you feel you need to strengthen for yourself.

For each segment of the wheel, ask the question, "How satisfied are you in this area of your life?" The center of the wheel is 0, which means "not satisfied," and the outer edge, 10, means "extremely satisfied." Rank your level of satisfaction with each life area by drawing a straight or curved line in each section to create a new outer edge. The new perimeter represents your Wheel of Life. How bumpy would the ride be if this were a real wheel?

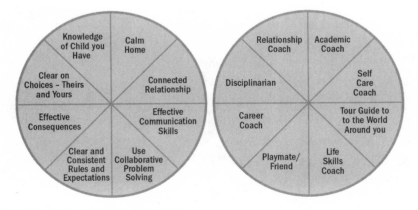

Fig. 8.3 Wheel of Life for Parents

Once the wheel is filled out, you can start to look at areas where you want to improve your level of satisfaction and think about what you might do to accomplish that. You don't necessar-・ily have to address the area that has the lowest score first, because work done in one area has an impact on every other area. Ask yourself a question like, "Which single action step, if I took it and did it consistently, would have the greatest effect on my life in this area?" Or you could choose one goal to work toward achieving in that area.

Concluding Thoughts

As you begin to make changes in how you parent and offer your child new ideas, supports, and opportunities, remember that change, for all involved, takes time. Things did not become challenging overnight, and success won't happen overnight either. Your child's behavior may even seem to get worse as you start implementing new rules and responding to her differently. She is no longer getting the response from you that she wants and that she's used to. She may escalate her negative behavior to get you to revert to something more familiar, more comfortable, and that allows for the status quo. Remember your *black belt* training. Recognize that even with all your efforts and theirs, there will still be those difficult times. Don't focus too much on these times. Let them pass; let them go. Focus on the tools and strategies you have to turn these times around.

If . . .

- You are confident that you have done all you can to engage your child in conversation, including making it clear that you are open to providing incentives rather than punishments, and have been unsuccessful having your child collaborate with you
- You fear violence or destruction
- You suspect anxiety, depression, drugs, or alcohol is playing a role in the resistance

- You believe that having an intermediary might help open the flow of conversation or help the two of you work through some of the disagreements

. . . then it may be helpful to seek the counsel of a trained parent coach or therapist. Be sure you seek out someone who is trained and knowledgeable about ADHD. See the Resources section for helpful websites.

Unfortunately, there are still many myths and misconceptions about ADHD that children—and adults—must contend with. Kids with ADHD are sometimes bullied or isolated, and parents often must fight their schools to receive services for their children. This makes it uncomfortable for some to seek the guidance and support they truly need. As Anderson Cooper said in Andrew Sullivan's blog (*The Dish*, July 2, 2012) regarding his own decision to publically acknowledge his *own* difference in being gay,

> While as a society we are moving toward greater inclusion and equality for all people, the tide of history only advances when people make themselves fully visible. My hope is that a more educated public will lead to such acceptance for all.

It's Time for Your Black Belt Test

As with all learning, repetition and review are vital in making sure that the lessons are not just understood, but remembered and integrated into your memory. I encourage you to take this review test as an opportunity to explore what you have learned and your commitment to the changes you will make. The answers can be found in Appendix E.

1. Maintain a _____ perspective. (Key 1)
2. Without _____ , no learning can take place. (Key 2)
3. _____ and _____ can shut some kids (and adults) down. (Key 2)

4. We cannot control _____ behavior, but we can control _____ . (Key 2)

5. The three steps of praise are _____ , _____ , and _____ . (Key 3)

6. Replace shame, blame, and criticism with _____ , _____ , and _____ . (Key 4)

7. Don't always take their behavior _____ (Key 4)

8. When reprimanding, Be _____ , Be _____ and Be _____ . (Key 4)

9. Kids do well ___ _____ ____ . If he could, he would. Parents do well ___ _____ ____ , too. (Key 5)

10. Challenging behaviors are due to either an _____ _____ or a _____ _____ _____ . (Key 5)

11. What are the three plans for approaching unmet expectations, and what do they represent?
Plan __ – _____
Plan __ – _____
Plan __ – _____ (Key 5)

12. What are the three steps in collaborative problem solving? _____ _____ , _____ _____ , and _____ _____ (Key 5)

13. Look for _____ , not _____ . (Key 5)

14. Strive to be _____ , but parent the _____ ____ _____. (Key 6)

15. To be responsible, first you must be _____ _____ . (Key 6)

16. In responding to their negative actions, R_____ , R_____ , R_____ , and R_____. (Key 7)

17. All we can give is information. It is their _____ . (Key 8)

18. Ultimately, _____ ____ responsible for their success and happiness. (Key 8)

Remember that at the core of ADHD is the struggle to regulate emotions and activity. Now that we have completed our home, you can clearly see the positive impact you can have in helping

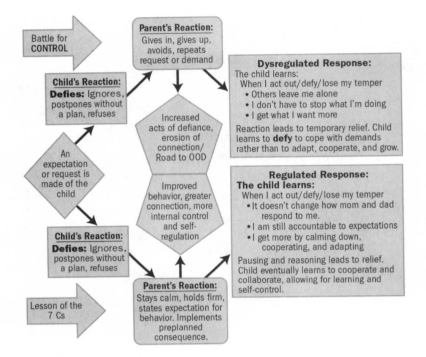

Fig. 8.4 Road to Self-Regulation

your kids improve their behavior by regulating their own emotional responses (Figure 8.4).

Once you can comfortably read and sign the certificate (Figure 8.5), you have earned your black belt. Remember, you are never alone in this journey. In the end, growing up happens. It just may take longer for the pieces to fall into place. In the meanwhile, buckle down, accept the traffic, and find your joy in the journey. Always give your child a sense of hope. Help her find her unique pathway to success!

Guiding Thoughts

- Be clear for yourself, and then to your child, whether she has a choice in what you are asking her to do or whether it is just your preference.

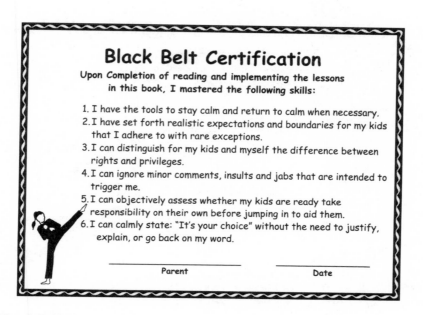

Black Belt Certification

Upon Completion of reading and implementing the lessons in this book, I mastered the following skills:

1. I have the tools to stay calm and return to calm when necessary.
2. I have set forth realistic expectations and boundaries for my kids that I adhere to with rare exceptions.
3. I can distinguish for my kids and myself the difference between rights and privileges.
4. I can ignore minor comments, insults and jabs that are intended to trigger me.
5. I can objectively assess whether my kids are ready take responsibility on their own before jumping in to aid them.
6. I can calmly state: "It's your choice" without the need to justify, explain, or go back on my word.

Parent   Date

Fig. 8.5 Black Belt Certificate

- All we can give is information. It is your child's choice what she does.
- You cannot always control your child's choices, but you can control how you respond to her choices.
- Be willing to detach yourself from your child's success or happiness in the moment.
- When possible, help raise your child's awareness of the choices she is making without shame, blame, or criticism.
- Speak out loud some of the choices you are making as you go through your day.
- Ask permission to support your child before actually supporting her.

Homework

1. Draw a picture of the completed home with *Calm, Connection, Communication, Collaboration, Clarity, Consistency, Consequences,*

and *Choices* written around it. If at any time you feel that things in your home are not going as you wish, pull out this picture and see where you need to begin your work.

2. Mark a date on your calendar to review the Guiding Thoughts in each chapter each month for the next five months. The reminder can help keep you accountable to the work you are doing to bring lasting changes to you and your family.

Appendix A: What is ADHD Coaching?

Coaching is a collaborative, action-oriented partnership designed to help people make the changes they want. ADHD Coaching is life coaching specifically designed to address the unique concerns of individuals who deal with the challenges of ADHD. A certified ADHD Coach is specially educated and trained in the research, science, and most effective treatment plans for working with people with ADHD, executive function disorders, and related issues.

Widely respected organizations and individuals, including the National Institute of Mental Health, Children and Adults with Attention Deficit Disorder (CHADD), Russell Barkley (*ADHD: A Handbook for Diagnosis and Treatment*), and Edward Hallowell (*Driven to Distraction*) have endorsed Coaching as a vital missing link for achieving success for individuals who have ADHD.

Appendix B: IEP and 504 Plan

If your child is struggling in school as a result of his ADHD, you may want to research which formal services or supports are available. While some services can be offered without a formal agreement with the school, your child may qualify and benefit from a specific service agreement. There are two legal avenues available:

504 PLAN
A **504 plan** is a legal document based on the provisions Section 504 of the Rehabilitation Act of 1973 that prohibits discrimination based upon disability. A disability is considered a physical or mental impairment that "substantially limits one or more major life activities" such as: learning, speaking, listening, reading, writing, concentrating, caring for oneself, etc. If your child is struggling to learn in an educational setting because of his ADHD, he may qualify for the 504 plan. This plan will specify the modifications and accommodations provided to your child so that he would have an opportunity perform at the same level as his peers.

INDIVIDUALIZED EDUCATIONAL PLAN (IEP)
The **Individualized Educational Plan (IEP)** is a written document that describes the goals, services, modifications, and accommodations a student would receive, if qualified, in the school setting. The IEP is mandated by the Individuals with Disabilities Education Act (IDEA). Under IDEA there are specific categories of disabilities. ADHD falls into the classification of "Other Health Impaired" (OHI).

For more information regarding the process of qualifying and advocating for these services, I recommend the following resources:

CHADD (www.CHADD.org)
Wrightslaw (www.wrightslaw.com)
ADDitude Magazine (www.ADDitudemag.com)

Appendix C: Accommodations and Modifications

Here is a list of some of the accommodations and modifications your kid may benefit from in each of the main areas of schooling. In some cases, you may be able to have the school provide these services through an IEP or 504 Plan. If your child does not qualify, then some of these may serve as suggestions and recommendations that you and the teacher can discuss providing more informally.

LEARN AND MASTER TOOLS AND TECHNIQUES NECESSARY
FOR PEAK LEARNING AND PERFORMANCE

- Efficient and rapid keyboarding skills.
- Use of computer graphic organizer program.
- Use of effective homework and assignment tracking system.
- Master planning of long-term assignments by creating short term assignments and due dates.
- System for actively turning in completed assignments.
- Use of blank card or other device to aid in tracking and reduce distractions for written material.
- Knowledge of multiple strategies for note taking, studying, and quiz/test taking to help student discover their preferred method.
- Use of timer to stay on task and budget time.

Active Learning

- Provide class notes to allow for additional focus during lesson time and to support at home learning and studying.
- Provide a study partner for added learning through discussion and modeling.
- Reinforce positive behaviors with specific praise to help with motivation and positive mindset.
- Provide reading material that is appropriate and stimulating with consideration for both fluency and comprehension levels. Explore audio books if appropriate.
- Highlight important information and material.

Working Memory aids

- Provide written instruction for classwork and homework.
- Allow use of calculator, formula sheets, and rule sheets.
- Provide visual aids for multiple step projects and activities.

Organization

- Color Code materials for each subject.
- Direct support for developing effective organization of materials, including multiple subject materials management and systems for remembering materials for home and school.

Attention and Behavior

- Discuss seat assignment with student to minimize distractions and maximize teacher support.
- Post classroom rules and schedules to aid in compliance and transitions.
- Develop discreet plan and signal with student for when student is distracted or off task.

- Develop discreet plan and signal with student for times when movement or less distracting environment is needed.
- Prepare for transition time with ample warning and transition plan.

STUDENT OUTPUT

- Give quizzes and tests to student alone or in small group.
- Allow extra time for assignments, quizzes, and tests.
- Allow short breaks during testing.
- Administer tests over multiple sessions.
- Provide interval time goals for longer assignments, quizzes and tests.
- Reduce distractions with study carrel.
- Remind for review of grammar and spelling.
- Allow for use of word processor to aid in speed and legibility of output.
- Allow for use of dictation software or other means of presenting information.
- Modify length of assignments when possible.
- Allow for white noise or headphones during independent work to reduce auditory distractions.
- Provide alternate method of demonstrating knowledge and skills.
- Allow student to write answers directly on test rather than Scantron.
- When possible, reduce the writing required by student and do not require rote copying of material from other sources.

ADDITIONAL SUPPORTS

- Adjust scheduling of classes so that classes that require the most mental focus are during student's peak learning time.
- Parent collaboration and communication.

◊ Have open communication with parent and student together about agreements and arrangements made with student regarding strategies and supports for staying on task, organizing, completing work, etc. so that parent can support and reinforce efforts at home.

◊ Maintain communication log (via notebook or email) with parent and students regarding goals, progress, and performance.

- Meet with student quarterly to set goals for performance (behavior, homework completion, quality of work), not just grades. This will allow student to adjust efforts and improve quality of performance.

- Provide a breakdown of the grade to show performance on content, grammar, process, etc..

- Age appropriate discussion of how learning challenges impact the student.

- Training and education for teacher regarding student's profile and challenges.

Appendix D: Letter to Request Services

When you apply for accommodations and services, your first step is to send a letter to the head of your district's special education department. Be prepared to provide any documentation that might support your request, including any doctor's diagnosis, school work, or communication with your child's teacher(s). You may also request that the school conduct appropriate assessments. If your child is going to be tested, you must sign a consent form allowing them to do so.

You should either hand deliver the letter or send it via certified mail for documentation of the date it was received since they will be required to take action within 60 days once they have been notified of your request.

Here is a sample of a letter you may use to request evaluation by your school:

REQUEST FOR EVALUATIONS AND PARENT REFERRAL LETTER TO CSE

[Date]

[Name of Committee on Special Education (CSE) Chairperson]
[School District]
[School Address]

Dear [Name of Committee on Special Education (CSE) Chairperson]:

[My/our] child, [child's name] is in [grade level] grade at [school name]. [I/we] believe that [s/he] might need special education services. The following difficulties support my/our concerns: [briefly list your concerns]

We request that the school district evaluate [child's name] under the Individuals with Disabilities Education Act (IDEA) to see if [s/he] has a disability and if services are necessary. [I/we] understand that these evaluations must be completed within 60 school days.

Please consider this a letter of referral to the CSE. [I/we] will need my copies of all written evaluations prior to the CSE meeting.

[I/we] look forward to talking with you about [child's name]. You can send [me/us] information or call [me/us] during the day at [daytime telephone number]. Thank you for your prompt attention to this request.

Sincerely,
[Your name(s)]
[Street Address]
[City, State, Zip Code]

cc: [Building Principal]

Appendix E: Answers to the Black Belt Test

1. Disability
2. Calm
3. Stress, Pressure
4. Their, Our
5. Notice, Name, Nurture
6. Tolerance, Empathy, Support
7. Personally
8. Brief, Firm, Gone
9. If they can, If they can
10. Unsolved problem, lagging thinking skill
11. A-Adult, B-Both, C-Child
12. Kid's Concern, Adult Concern, Brainstorm Solution
13. Conversations, Confrontations
14. Consistent, Child YOU have
15. Response Able
16. Reflect, Review, Redo, Respond
17. Choice
18. They are

Resources

With all of the websites and books available now on the topic of ADHD, it can be overwhelming to find helpful and accurate information. Here is a list of several of the websites, magazines and books I find most helpful in understanding and treating ADHD.

Websites

ADHD AWARENESS MONTH
Each year during the month of October, several prominent organizations coordinate their efforts to promote education and awareness of ADHD. This website has excellent resources that can be printed and distributed and is available all year long. (www.adhdawareness.org)

CHADD
The premier national non-profit organization that provides education, advocacy and support for individuals with ADHD. They have local chapters across the United States and in other parts of the world that provide ongoing support for parents and adults. In addition, they have an annual conference open to everyone where the top researchers and providers gather along with individuals impacted by ADHD to discuss the latest research and treatment. (www .chadd.org)

PTS COACHING
This is my website. Here you will find articles and resources for parents, students and educators. Please feel free to print and dis-

tribute anything you feel will be valuable in raising awareness of those who interact with your child. (www.PTScoaching.com)

PTS COACHING FACEBOOK PAGE
I post current research, articles, and resources on a regular basis. (https://www.facebook.com/PTSCoaching)

THINK:KIDS
Think:Kids provides training and support for kids who struggle with behavior based on the evidence-based Collaborative Problem Solving approach. (http://thinkkids.org/)

ADHD COACHES ORGANIZATION
The ADHD Coaches Organization is a non-profit association created to advance the profession of ADHD coaching worldwide. They serve as a resource for individuals to find qualified ADHD coaches. (http://www.adhdcoaches.org/)

NATIONAL RESOURCE CENTER ON ADHD
A division of CHADD, this organization provides ADHD science, information, resources, support. (http://help4adhd.org/)

LEARNING DISABILITIES ASSOCIATION OF AMERICA
Excellent resource for parents and educators on a wide range of learning disabilities (http://ldaamerica.org/)

NATIONAL CENTER FOR LEARNING DISABILITIES
Excellent resource for parents and educators on a wide range of learning disabilities (http://www.ncld.org/)

THE INTERNATIONAL DYSLEXIA ASSOCIATION
This organization has vast resources for individuals with dyslexia as well as for parents and educators. (http://interdys.org/)

WRIGHTS LAW

This site deals with Education Law and Advocacy. It is an excellent resource for parents, educators, advocates and attorneys. (http://wrightslaw.com/)

ATTENTION DEFICIT DISORDER ASSOCIATION

This organization provides information, resources and networking opportunities to help adults with Attention Deficit/ Hyperactivity Disorder (AD/HD) lead better lives.

MAGAZINES

Additude Magazine (http://www.additudemag.com/)

Attention Magazine – Provided as a membership benefit for joining CHADD (http://www.chadd.org)

BOOKS

Between Parent & Child by Haim G. Ginot

Between Parent & Teenager by Haim G. Ginot

CHADD *Educator's Manual* published by and available through CHADD

Change Your Questions, Change Your Life by Marilee Adams

Driven To Distraction by Edward Hallowell

Empowering Youth with ADHD: Your Guide to Coaching Adolescents and Young Adults for Coaches, Parents, and Professionals by Jodi Sleeper-Triplett MCC SCAC.

The Explosive Child: A New Approach for Understanding and Parenting Easily Frustrated, Chronically Inflexible Children by Ross Greene

Helping Your Anxious Child: A Step-by-Step Guide for Parents by Ronald Rapee PhD, Ann Wignall D Psych, Susan Spence PhD and Heidi Lyneham PhD

How to Win Friends and Influence People by Dale Carnegie

Life After High School: A Guide for Students With Disabilities and Their Families by Susan Yellin and Christina Cacioppo Bertsch

The Mindful Child: How to Help Your Kid Manage Stress and Become Happier, Kinder, and More Compassionate by Susan Kaiser Greenland

The Motivation Breakthrough by Richard Lavoie
Ready or Not Here Life Comes by Mel Levine
The 7 Habits of Highly Effective People by Stephen. R. Covey
Smart but Scattered by Peg Dawson and Richard Guare
Socially ADDept: Teaching Social Skills to Children with ADHD, LD, and Asperger's by Janet Z. Giler
My Thirteenth Winter: A memoir by Samantha Abeel
Worry by Edward Hallowell

BOOKS FOR KIDS EXPLAINING ADHD
All Dogs have ADHD by Kathy Hoopmann
Jimmy Racecar by J.B. Snyder
My Brain Needs Glasses: Living with Hyperactivity by Annick Vincent
My Friend the Trouble Maker: Learning to Focus and Thriving with ADHD by Rifka Schonfeld
Putting on the Brakes: Understanding and Taking Control of Your Add or ADHD by Patricia O. Quinn and Judith M. Stern
A Smart Girl's Guide to Knowing What to Say (American Girl) by Patti Kelley Criswell and Angela Martini
A Walk in the Rain with a Brain by Edward Hallowell

EXCELLENT KIDS SERIES WITH LEAD CHARACTERS
WHO HAVE ADHD/DYSLEXIA
Hank Zipzer: The World's Greatest Underachiever by Henry Winkler
Percy Jackson & the Olympians by Rick Riordan

References

Adams, M. G. (2009). *Change your questions, change your life: 10 powerful tools for life and work*. San Francisco, CA: Berrett-Koehler.

Barbaresi, W. J., Colligan, R. C., Weaver, A. L., Voigt, R. G., Killian, J. M., & Katusic, S. K. (2013). Mortality, ADHD, and psychosocial adversity in adults with childhood ADHD: A prospective study. *Pediatrics, 131*(4), 637–644. doi: 10.1542/peds.2012-2354

Barkley, R. A. (1990). *Attention-deficit hyperactivity disorder: A handbook for diagnosis and treatment*. New York: Guilford Press.

Barkley, R. A. (2000). *Taking charge of ADHD: The complete, authoritative guide for parents*. New York: Guilford Press.

Barkley, R. A. (2010). *Deficient Emotional Self-Regulation is a Core Component of ADHD: Evidence and Treatment Implications*.

Barkley, R. A., Edwards, G., & Robin, A. L. (1999). *Defiant teens: A clinician's manual for assessment and family intervention*. New York: Guilford Press.

Burke, J. D., Pardini, A., Lobber, R. (2008). Reciprocal relationships between parenting behavior and disruptive psychopathology from childhood through adolescence. *Journal of Abnormal Child Psychology, 36*(5), 679–692.

Bustamante, E. M. (2000). *Treating the disruptive adolescent: Finding the real child behind oppositional defiant disorders*. Northvale, NJ: Jason Aronson.

Covey, S. R. (1989). *The seven habits of highly effective people: Restoring the character ethic*. New York: Simon & Schuster.

CHADD National Conference, Atlanta, Nov. 12, 2010 Keynote presentation.

Dawson, P., & Guare, R. (2004). *Executive skills in children and adolescents: A practical guide to assessment and intervention*. New York: Guilford Press.

Dawson, P., & Guare, R. (2009). *Smart but scattered: The revolutionary "executive skills" approach to helping kids reach their potential*. New York: Guilford Press.

Diagnostic and statistical manual of mental disorders: DSM-5. (2013). Washington, DC: American Psychiatric Association.

Dweck, C. S. (2006). *Mindset: The new psychology of success.* New York: Random House.

Elia, J., Ambrosini, P., & Berrettini, W. (2008). ADHD characteristics: I. Concurrent co-morbidity patterns in children & adolescents. *Child and Adolescent Psychiatry and Mental Health, 2*(1), 15. doi: 10.1186/1753-2000-2-15

Faber, A., & Mazlish, E. (1974). *Liberated parents/liberated children.* New York: Grosset & Dunlap.

Fowler, M. C., Barkley, R. A., Reeve, R., & Zentall, S. (1995). *CH. A.D.D. educators manual: An in-depth look at attention deficit disorders from an educational perspective: A project of the CH. A.D.D. National Education Committee.* Plantation, FL: CH. A.D.D.

Galinsky, E. (n.d.). Inside the teenage brain [Interview transcript]. Retrieved from http://www.pbs.org/wgbh/pages/frontline/shows/teen brain/interviews/galinsky.html

Genomewide Association Studies: History, Rationale, and Prospects for Psychiatric Disorders. (2009). *American Journal of Psychiatry, 166*(5), 540-556. doi: 10.1176/appi.ajp.2008.08091354

Ginott, H. G. (1969). *Between parent and teenager.* New York: Macmillan.

Giwerc, D. (2011). *Permission to proceed: The keys to creating a life of passion, purpose and possibility for adults with ADHD.* New York: ADD Coach Academy.

Glasser, H., & Easley, J. (1998). *Transforming the difficult child: The nurtured heart approach.* Tucson, AZ: Center for the Difficult Child Publications.

Glasser, W. (1998). Choice theory: A new psychology of personal freedom. New York: HarperCollins.

Greene, R. W. (1998). *The explosive child: A new approach for understanding and parenting easily frustrated, "chronically inflexible" children.* New York: HarperCollins.

Greenland, S. K. (2010). *The mindful child: How to help your kid manage stress and become happier, kinder, and more compassionate.* New York: Free Press.

Hallowell, E. M., & Ratey, J. J. (1995). *Driven to distraction: Recognizing and coping with attention deficit disorder from childhood through adulthood.* New York: Simon & Schuster.

Keirsey, D., & Bates, M. M. (1984). *Please understand me: Character &*

temperament types. Del Mar, CA: Distributed by Prometheus Nemesis Book.

Lavoie, R. D. (2007). *The motivation breakthrough: 6 secrets to turning on the tuned-out child*. New York: Touchstone.

Learning Disabilities Association of America. (n.d.). Retrieved from http://ldaamerica.org/

Levine, M. D. (2005). *Ready or not, here life comes*. New York: Simon & Schuster.

McCann, C. (2012, January 26). New research on behavior and academic achievement in kindergarten. Retrieved from http://earlyed .newamerica.net/blogposts/2012/new_research_on_behavior_and_ academic_achievement_in_kindergarten-62862

Minahan, J., & Rappaport, N. (2012). *The behavior code: A practical guide to understanding and teaching the most challenging students*. Cambridge, MA: Harvard Education Press.

Minahan, J., & Rappaport, N. (2012). *The behavior code: A practical guide to understanding and teaching the most challenging students*. Cambridge, MA: Harvard Education Press.

Mischke-Reeds, M. (2015). *8 keys to practicing mindfulness: Practical strategies for emotional health and well-being*. New York: Norton.

MTA Cooperative Group. (1999). A 14-month randomized clinical trial of treatment strategies for attention deficit hyperactivity disorder. *Archives of General Psychiatry, 56,* 12.

National Resource Center on ADHD. (n.d.). Retrieved from http:// help4adhd.org/

Nigg, J. T. (2006). *What causes ADHD?: Understanding what goes wrong and why*. New York: Guilford Press.

Pink, D. H. (2009). *Drive: The surprising truth about what motivates us*. New York, NY: Riverhead Books.

Ratey, J. J., & Hagerman, E. (2008). *Spark: The revolutionary new science of exercise and the brain*. New York: Little, Brown.

Rogers, C. R. (1961). *On becoming a person: A therapist's view of psychotherapy*. Boston: Houghton Mifflin Company.

Rosenberg, M. B. (2003). *Nonviolent communication: A language of life*. Encinitas, CA: PuddleDancer Press.

Sleeper-Triplett, J. (2010). *Empowering youth with ADHD: Your guide to coaching adolescents and young adults for coaches, parents, and professionals*. Plantation, FL: Specialty Press.

Think:Kids. "Collaborative Problem Solving." (n.d.). Retrieved from http://thinkkids.org/

Wolf, A. E. (1991). *Get out of my life, but first could you drive me and Cheryl to the mall?: A parent's guide to the new teenager*. New York: Noonday Press.

Ziegler Dendy, C.A., & Zeigler, A. (2003). *A bird's-eye view of life with ADD and ADHD: Advice from young survivors! A reference book for children and teenagers*. Cedar Bluff, AL: Cherish the Children.

Index

Note: Page locators accompanied by *f* indicate figure.

Also available from the
8 Keys to Mental Health Series

8 Keys to Raising the Quirky Child:
How to Help a Kid Who Doesn't (Quite) Fit In
Mark Bowers

8 Keys to Eliminating Passive-Aggressiveness
Andrea Brandt

8 Keys to Forgiveness
Robert Enright

8 Keys to Recovery from an Eating Disorder:
Effective Strategies from Therapeutic Practice and Personal Experience
Carolyn Costin, Gwen Schubert Grabb

8 Keys to Building Your Best Relationships
Daniel A. Hughes

8 Keys to Old School Parenting for Modern-Day Families
Michael Mascolo

8 Keys to Practicing Mindfulness:
Practical Strategies for Emotional Health and Well-Being
Manuela Mischke Reeds

8 Keys to Safe Trauma Recovery:
Take-Charge Strategies to Empower Your Healing
Babette Rothschild

8 Keys to Brain-Body Balance
Robert Scaer

8 Keys to Stress Management
Elizabeth Anne Scott

8 Keys to End Bullying:
Strategies for Parents & Schools
Signe Whitson